D0064863

QUEST FOR KAITIAKITANGA

THE ANCIENT MĀORI SECRET FROM NEW ZEALAND
THAT COULD SAVE THE EARTH

RICHARD BANGS

MENASHA RIDGE PRESS

Cover design by Travis Bryant
Text design by Annie Long
Cover photograph courtesy of Tourism New Zealand
Author photograph by John Canning
Other photographs:
   Walker Bangs, pages 4, 14, 15, 19, 58, 65, 71, 76, 154, 216
   Sara Givens, pages 8, 23, 33, 103, 104, 215, 221
   Laura Hubber, pages xii, 94
   Didrik Johnck, pages 6, 31, 32, 55, 79, 85, 97, 111, 159, 160, 181, 182, 198, 211, 212, 219
   Small World Productions, pages 34, 37, 42, 63, 108, 118, 128, 150, 205
   Sally Solaro, page 176
   Tourism New Zealand, pages 11, 24, 47, 82, 123, 127, 130, 133, 136, 139, 147, 165, 175, 185, 228
Indexing by Sylvia Coates

Library of Congress Cataloging-in-Publication Data

Bangs, Richard, 1950–
   Quest for Kaitiakitanga: the ancient Māori secret from New Zealand
that could save the Earth/by Richard Bangs.
   p. cm.
   Includes index.
   ISBN-13: 978-0-89732-658-2
   ISBN-10: 0-89732-658-X
   1. New Zealand—Description and travel. 2. Bangs, Richard, 1950–, —Travel—
New Zealand. 3. Philosophy, Māori. 4. Māori (New Zealand people)—Religion.
5. Māori (New Zealand people)—Social life and customs. 6. Human ecology—
New Zealand. 7. Nature—Effect of human beings on—New Zealand. 8. New Zealand—
Environmental conditions. 9. Sustainable development—New Zealand—Philosophy.
   I. Title.

DU413.B36 2008
993—dc22
                                    2007047830

Menasha Ridge Press
P.O. Box 43673
Birmingham, Alabama 35243
www.menasharidge.com

table *of* contents

Acknowledgments v

Foreword viii

Introduction 1

CHAPTER ONE: *Deep Float* 7

CHAPTER TWO: *Prophet Motive* 12

CHAPTER THREE: *Scotch on the Rocks* 20

CHAPTER FOUR: *Uncommon Currency* 30

CHAPTER FIVE: *Less Bad Is Good* 39

CHAPTER SIX: *Tart Imitating Life* 45

CHAPTER SEVEN: *Hell Freezes Over* 52

CHAPTER EIGHT: *I Need All the Alp I Can Get* 56

CHAPTER NINE: *Immaculate Confection* 72

CHAPTER TEN: *Tall Tails* 80

CHAPTER ELEVEN: *A Time to Krill* 92

CHAPTER TWELVE: *Adventures with Porpoise* 101

CHAPTER THIRTEEN: *Like Nothing but Itself* 109

CHAPTER FOURTEEN: *The Price of Emissions* 114

CHAPTER FIFTEEN: *Not Less than Everything* 119

CHAPTER SIXTEEN: *There's a Fjord in Your Future* 124

CHAPTER SEVENTEEN: *Wheels of Fortune* 134

CHAPTER EIGHTEEN: *Power Lunch* 140

CHAPTER NINETEEN:

One Touch of Nature Makes the Whole World Kin. 148

CHAPTER TWENTY: *Moa's Ark*. 155

CHAPTER TWENTY-ONE: *Just the Flax, Ma'am* 166

CHAPTER TWENTY-TWO: *River Dance* 169

CHAPTER TWENTY-THREE: *Shear Madness* 179

CHAPTER TWENTY-FOUR: *Man Bites Planet*. 193

CHAPTER TWENTY-FIVE: *The Prime Truth* 202

CHAPTER TWENTY-SIX: *Stop Making Sense*. 208

CHAPTER TWENTY-SEVEN: *Cosmosis* 217

CHAPTER TWENTY-EIGHT: *End of the Line* 224

Index 253

About the Author 261

ACKNOWLEDGMENTS

A magic journey such as this takes a ship of many people, and I hoist flags here to but a few:

First, I want to thank Sir Edmund Hillary for his generous granting of his time and support, and Prime Minister Helen Clark for same. Everett Peirce, father of Tom, helped set this in motion with his unmitigated love for New Zealand. Paul Maritz oiled the engine with his views and explorations.

I want to call out Ian Murray, of whom there is no greater enthusiast for all things New Zealand, and who was my guide and muse throughout; and my son, Walker T. Bangs, who joined us and turned rocks I did not see.

Drawing from my imperfect memory and notes, I want to acknowledge, in a stab at alphabetical order, the many who helped me in New Zealand with time, advice, wisdom, logistics, dags, and understanding:

Alex Ewing of Aspiring Helicopters; Alister Brown and Steve Logan of Logan Brown Restaurant & Bar; Andrew B. Luke, trustee for Ngāti Rārua Ātiawa Iwi Trust; Annette Main, John Blythe, and Billy the Kid of The Flying Fox; Baldy Haitana, Whanganui master guide; Bill Hamilton of Kai in the City; Bruce Lahood of Tourism New Zealand; Chris Tobias, former sustainable business development manager for Green Globe New Zealand; Craig and Pip Gibson, directors of Orakei Korako Cave and Thermal Park; Dr. Dan Rollinson, resident ecologist at Ngā Kaitiaki; Ed Sims, group general manager international airline at Air New Zealand; Gavin Wills, a great adventurer and inspiration; Grant Harnish of Salt Air; Hekenukumai "Hector" Busby; Hijiri Kitamura, the great South Island Māori guide; Jim Hill, CEO of NETCOR and Wairakei Terraces; John Barrett and Minnie Clark of Kapiti Island Alive; John Panoho of Navigator

Tours; Jon Hamilton, river pioneer; Joyce Conrad-Munns, guide and wise one; Jude Dods of Kura Contemporary Ethnic Art; Karen Laugesen of Air New Zealand; Kauahi Ngapora, operations manager for Whale Watch; Kevin Heays, mayor of Kaikoura; Koro Carman, managing director for Crossing Hokianga; Kylie Ruwhiu-Karawana, Māori development manager for Tourism New Zealand; Linda and Simon Pharazyn of the Fyffe View Ranch; Lindsay Kain of Haast River Safaris; Lucinda Ducker of Taipa Bay Resort; Marie Coburn of Franz Josef Glacier Country Retreat; Maurice and Heather Manawatu of Māori Tours Kaikoura; Neroli Gold, manager of Kaikoura Winery; Niko Tangaroa of Waka Tours; Noriko Burra of Trees for Travellers; Paul Aubrey, chief guide for Adventure Consultants; Pauline and Hāmi Te Rākau of Awatuna Homestead; Raewyn Tan of Positively Wellington Tourism; Richard Miller of the Stone Lodge; Ricky Pincott of Mud Cycles; Roger North, builder of Wanaka Homestead; Sarah Keenan of Tourism New Zealand; Shaun Murdoch of Fergs Kayaks; Stephen King of the Waipoua Forest Trust; Steve Gill, The Tree Guy; Steve Lafferty of Bayview Wairakei Resort; Steve Moffat, expedition leader for Adventure Consultants; Stevie Wall of Kaitiaki Adventures; Susan Gibson of the Heritage Auckland Hotel; Tess Hellebrekers of Lake Wanaka Tourism; Tina Cook at Te Papa Tongarewa, Museum of New Zealand; and last but in no way least, Vanessa Mutu of Tourism New Zealand.

And I'd like to thank Bart Henderson, who was the first Sobek guide to New Zealand, and John Kramer, who joined me there soon thereafter.

And Carey Peterson, who helped with research and transcribing. She is the scaffolding of my books.

I want to give special thanks to Mountain Travel Sobek for its continued vision and keenness for all New Zealand adventures, and in particular to Nadia LeBon, Kevin Callaghan, Kim Beck, and Anne Wood.

And there can be no adventure taken without ExOfficio, the brand of exceptional clothing and gear I have been wearing and punishing to no effect for more than twenty years now. And that goes for my luggage of choice, Eagle Creek, and my tireless footwear from Teva.

Also, I want to thank AdventureLink (and founders Kelly Tompkins and Michael Culhane), which through its galaxy of outfitters offers a number of great trips to New Zealand; Anupam Gupta of Mixpo, who helped showcase our online media; the ATTA (Adventure Travel Trade Association), which helped with contacts and support; and Dick Schulte and the team at Adventure Central.

And an overflowing dollop of gratitude to David Kleinman and Shantini Ramakrishnan of Spring, O'Brien, friends to whom I turned for all manner of guidance and insight.

A big-screen-sized thanks needs to go to the incredible film crew that captured this odyssey for public television and beyond. It includes executive producer John Givens; director-writer Patty Conroy; cinematographer extraordinaire Karel Bauer; super adventure videographer Didrik Johnck; grip and production coordinator Sara Givens; genius editor-composer-graphics guy and super hyphenate-talent David Ris; American Public Television executives Nelsa Gidney and Chris Funkhouser for believing in, distributing, and promoting *Adventures with Purpose* documentaries to the stations; and of course my compass, producer-writer-director, mastermind, moral supporter, and muse, Laura Hubber.

And I want to thank the team at Menasha Ridge Press, including Howard Cohen, Molly Merkle, Tricia Parks, and my wise and talented editor, Russell Helms. My gratitude also to copyeditor Steve Millburg.

FOREWORD

We all dream of adventures. Author and world explorer Richard Bangs actually lives them. This unique and remarkable man has experienced firsthand the wonders of untraveled rivers and wild mountains, and he has been fortunate to get up close and personal with the people who've dedicated their lives to caring and protecting them.

Through the time I've spent with Richard, I've come to understand that it isn't about the conquest or the triumph but the journey itself, the discoveries and the relationships made along the way. In my life I am fortunate to have come into contact with many people who have and continue to dedicate their lives to making the world a better place. As my interest in these people and their work has grown, so too has my awareness of our environment and the importance of its conservation. As a messenger through the media, my life's work is to ignite the passion and respect for the earth that we will leave to our children in an effort to sustain our natural resources for the generations to come.

Richard has just completed a comprehensive tour of Aotearoa, or New Zealand. His aim has been to discover and reveal the passion New Zealanders have for preserving and maintaining what makes this country truly unique.

Buoyed by the forward thinking of Kiwis, Richard ventured to their homeland, climbing its mountains, running its rivers, kayaking its seas, and spending time with almost everyone he encountered along the way. During his travels, he discovered how the country's commitment to sustainability is playing a vital role in placing New Zealand at the forefront of earth-friendly resource use and management. He discovered not only a renewed movement to preserve what is special and essential about New Zealand but also how, as a nation, they are working hard toward improving the country for generations to come. His gift to New Zealand in return for exploring the beauty of this land and its people, is this book and his perspective.

In the pages that follow, I think you will take great pleasure and interest not only in Richard's wanderings but his carefully researched findings. He embraces wholeheartedly New Zealand and its people, sharing their stories and legends. Our best hopes for the future are a strong and well-informed public and those devoted people who work so tirelessly to improve the world around them.

Perhaps still not completely understood by those with classically trained eyes and ears, the Māori concept of *kaitiakitanga,* or guardianship, as interpreted by Richard, allows a pay-it-forward sensibility and bares New Zealand as a model perhaps for the whole of the world. I invite you to join this trek—it might just change your perspective and make a difference for us all.

—*Debbie Levin*
President, Environmental Media Association

INTRODUCTION

f travel is about a colliding of realities, it is no less about the breeding of illusions: romance, adventure, and promise; greener pastures; secret answers; and peoples more splendid than ourselves. But as I've grabbed more than a fair helping of traveling the world in my career, I've also undergone a quiet erosion of these illusions.

Just when my spirit was at its lowest, my close friend Tom Peirce guided me to an odyssey that gave me renewed optimism and excitement, not to mention a whole new concept for living in accord with the planet. It was a wonderful, precious gift—and, as it turned out, Tom's last.

Not long before this revelation, I traveled through Africa, a continent I first visited in 1973 and to which I have returned many times. With me were two African scholars, Paul Maritz, who was born in then-Rhodesia (now Zimbabwe) and has invested significantly in ways to improve the lot of Africans, and Dr. Emmanuel Akyeampong, a Ghanaian-born professor of history at Harvard University.

As we stood above a palm-fringed quay on the Gold Coast of West Africa, on the fusty ramparts of a fifteenth-century slave castle, Emmanuel talked about how the slave trade stole some of the most physically fit, leaving behind the infirm to procreate. He said it forced tribes into hiding in infertile areas, where they grew cassava and other not-especially-nourishing foods, affecting the well-being of subsequent generations. Families were torn apart. Social mores and traditions were washed out to sea. What remained was a culture of fear. Today, many

Opposite *The author and team running Tutea Falls, a sheer twenty-three-foot drop, the steepest vertical commercially run waterfall in the world*

1

young Africans don't know the history that has shaped their lot, and so they assume a self-perpetuating fatalism and ambivalence. Young Africans are often puzzled and unsure, their vision of a future flat.

From Ghana we traveled southeast to Mozambique, a country still reeling in the wake of Cyclone Eline in 2000, which left half a million people homeless and killed 70 percent of the livestock in some provinces.

When the storm hit, Mozambique had only recently emerged from a seventeen-year civil war in which an externally financed movement called RENAMO set out to destroy the Marxist government and wreak wholesale destruction on the social and communications infrastructure. Schools, clinics, roads, and railways were all ruined. During this period, RENAMO killed an estimated one hundred thousand Mozambicans in what the U.S. State Department called "one of the most brutal holocausts against ordinary human beings since World War II." Many were killed by the land mines salted throughout the country, and still today we cannot drive or hike off established routes for fear of being blown to pieces.

Crossing the border into Zimbabwe, which was enjoying more than 2,000 percent annual inflation, I was shaken down for a bribe, the fiddle being that the visa I had secured minutes before was invalid. That of course was nothing compared to the fate of my friend Justin Seymour-Smith, whose family for generations had run a quiet farm and wildlife park that featured one of the last populations of endangered rhinos. Under the policies of Zimbabwe's president, Robert Mugabe, Justin's family property was confiscated, much of the wildlife was shot for food, and the Seymour-Smith family was forced to flee with little more than the clothes on their backs.

Then we crossed to Botswana, to the Northern Tuli Game Reserve, which once harbored some of the greatest populations of big game in

Africa. Much of the area was flattened and dry, the shrub and grass cropped close to the ground. "This is a problem," the ranger pointed out. "This park is fenced.... We border two other countries, Zimbabwe and South Africa, and the animals can't cross the borders, can't follow their natural migrations. So they circulate in containment here, sometimes with devastating effects. Since I've been here we've lost five plant species to the elephants."

On the way back, I made a road trip through Serbia, Bosnia, and Croatia, and couldn't ignore the great disfiguring swaths of clear-cut forest, scars across a green countenance of hundred-year-old pines and beech. The political thunderstorms that have crashed over the Balkans for millennia have not been kind to these vast natural assets, especially of late. Less than 1 percent of the area is protected, but even that is a dubious designation. The war ended more a dozen years ago, but it left much of the region devastated economically and, some would say, morally. In the rush to find a new economy, the land is being skinned at record rates, usually for nonsustainable, short-term benefits, often illicitly. Every hour of the day, belching diesel trucks bearing timber, some of it from irreplaceable primary forest, trundled past me on the way to Italy or other hardwoods markets. What would be left for my sons, or their own children, to wonder at?

Soon afterward, I headed to Central America to kayak Lago de Nicaragua, host to the only freshwater sharks in the world. But I saw no sharks and found that the lake has become treacherously polluted. Worse, I learned that more than half of Nicaraguans don't have access to basic services for drinking water, a travesty in a land of rain forests, huge natural lakes, and many rivers. When I then returned to Indonesia after an absence of ten years, my old friend Dr. Halim Indrakusuma bemoaned how the environmental integrity of his country had plunged. He talked

Tom Peirce and the author

about a drilling accident in East Java that released a torrent of toxic mud, leveling villages and leaving ten thousand homeless. He said that in ten years, Indonesia, once the cabinet of Asia with its vast forests of hardwood, would have to import timber.

Then, to throw another treated log onto the fire of disenchantment, I took an opportunity to dive in Fiji, where the coral is etiolating to the color of a bathtub.

I shared many of these moments with Tom Peirce as he lay in a hospital bed in his hometown of Aspen, Colorado. Tom had started an adventure-travel company, High Country Passage, not long after I founded Sobek, and over the years we had swapped many, many stories of adventure and the lyric joys of travel. We had compared notes and contacts and insights, and shared the canoe in which we ran the shoals of businesses that showcased wonder. But now Tom was stricken with a most unkind jolt—lung cancer, though he didn't smoke—and he wondered if the cause might have somehow been environmental.

"The world seems to be getting worse," I lamented.

"Yeah. But there is an exception," his said, his eyes sharpening. "New Zealand. It keeps getting better."

Tom's father, Everett, owned a holiday home in New Zealand. Every year, he and Tom would make a visit to fly-fish, hike, and explore.

"You need to go back and take a look. It will give you hope," Tom advised. His words tugged at the levers of my soul.

A few weeks later, Tom underwent experimental therapy in a city where the heron is the official bird, Portland, Oregon. Before the procedure was done, Tom, like a migratory bird, was gone.

And I decided to go back to New Zealand.

DEEP FLOAT

He manga wai koia kia kore e whitikia.

It is a big river indeed that cannot be crossed.

have always successfully resisted the impulse to surrender when it comes to running white water. As a guide with some years of experience, I know how to read water and feel confident about my own skills—and limitations. I've lived and survived by the adage shared with me by an explorer in Sumatra some years ago: "Love many, trust few. Always paddle your own canoe."

But this is something requiring a new paradigm for me. Part of adventure is the refusal to be dissuaded by the thought of one's own demise; another is putting faith in the unknown. I am tucked into the bottom of a frail coffin of a raft, arms stretched to

The author rolling on the river—the River Kaituna, which means "fish food" in local parlance. It drains Lake Rotoiti, making a tremendous fuss in a series of flashing leaps in its tear to the sea.

ropes, hands in death grips around the strands, my blue-bladed paddle pressed flat against the tube, useless as a tool for navigation. In the back, a young Māori man, his ponytail flying, is hollering something a bit foreboding over the roar: "Be strong. Be brave. Be stout-hearted."

I've agreed to cede control to someone less than half my age who has a wild look in his eye and works with a company whose name I cannot pronounce, let alone translate: Kaitiaki Adventures. Ahead I can see the tops of trees at eye level on the near horizon, a harbinger I know too well. We are on the Class V Kaituna River, a sprint of a watercourse that spins near the boiling mud pools and hell-like geysers of Rotorua in the midsection of the North Island of New Zealand. We are caroming toward Tutea Falls, a sheer twenty-three-foot drop, the steepest vertical fall over which I have willingly agreed to plunge in my long boating career.

As the river speeds to the edge, time seems to slow, then go quiet, wrapping us in its cloth. Always in river mechanics there are elements of indeterminacy simply beyond rational comprehension, and my mind goes on standby with this ride. The current rises like the back of a snake. The gorge is dark, with treetops on either bank touching in the middle, covering us with what seems like a rotting tarpaulin. Towering red podocarps stud the banks with mélanges of green, delicate leaves; ferns hang in festoons; underbrush clutters the banks in luxuriant, unrepentant profusion. Over us hangs a brooding, watching silence, like a predatory bird. We are sailing straight into the eye of a god.

Just minutes earlier at the put-in, our guide had explained in excited cadence a bit about our raftabout. The River Kaituna, which means "fish food" in local parlance, drains Lake Rotoiti, making a tremendous fuss in a series of flashing leaps in its tear to the sea. It boasts the biggest drop of any commercially rafted waterfall in the world. There are three waterfalls among the fourteen rapids, but the last, known to Māori as Okere, which simply means "waterfall," is the prize. It brooks no debate in its cascade.

This section of river was valued long before rafters plied it, as it was the site of the first hydroelectric power station to supply a township in New Zealand. It was also a sacred cemetery and a hideout during various tribal wars; behind and around the waterfall are caves that once harbored women and children, caves that blink with the light of millions of glowworms.

The rafting concern is Māori-owned, and one of the guides explains that the translation of the company name—Kaitiaki—is "guardian" or "caretaker." He sweeps his hand in a broad arc and continues: "Māori believe everything around us is alive: the sky, the mountains, the river. And so we are *kaitiaki* of this place, and before we head downstream we like to pay proper respect."

He bows his head and presses his fingertips to his lips, and in the most euphonic tongue he recites a *karakia,* or traditional Māori prayer:

> *E hōnore, he korōria ki te Atua.*
> *He maungarongo ki te whenua.*
> *He whakaaro pai ki ngā tangata katoa.*
> *Amine.*

> Glory to the highest.
> Peace on earth.
> Good will to all mankind.
> Amen.

Minutes later we are approaching Tutea Falls, named for a Māori chief whose bones are hidden behind the curtain of falling water. Just above the drop we nose into Last Chance Eddy at a place where nature has been lavish with her paint. Among a medley of green, I pluck a silver fern leaf, as instructed by Stevie Wall, our pilot, a creature of pure sinew and purpose, more like an anatomist's drawing of a man than the real thing. For a second, I think I feel a current of power in this leaf. Stevie says I should toss it over my shoulder into the river—if it lands green side up, we will have safe passage over the waterfall; if it lands silver side up, we will capsize.

I make the toss and turn to watch as the leaf flutters and floats to the water's surface. It lands with a whisper, all shiny and lambent, flashing

Nature is New Zealand's leading artist—just four million inhabitants live in a country the size of Japan. A third of the land area is preserved within a network of parks and nature reserves, and there are forty thousand square kilometers of native forest. Come and explore this special part of the world, where nature is still in control of how things look and feel.

our future. Submitting to the moment, we tighten our life jackets and back-paddle into the current for the main descent. Then I assume the crouch in the bilge of the bow. The river seems to shiver with impatience.

Now, at the brink, the banks tighten like a funnel. There is a whoosh of wet air, and we hang for a stretched second at the threshold, then are hurled toward the horizon—down, down, down. A deadly silence seems to settle. We are enclosed in a lightless room. Then we are flying in foam, my helmet pressed with a fire hose of spray. There is a crackling from the aerated water, like the sound of torn air. Twisted, roiled, pulled, and folded, the raft seems to have turned over. But then with a lurch and a kick, we are spat to the other side, upright and free, and the canyon swells with whoops and the slap of paddles doing a high five.

At the takeout, the shore of an old philosophy, Stevie gathers the rafters to pay a final respect, a *waiata,* or song of the river. It is sung in Māori, but translates to "Our raft is peace. Our paddlers aboard come from the spring above. The reason for our gathering today is for friendship. May it be long and distant."

PROPHET MOTIVE

E te hihi o te ra e kokiri kei runga e,
Tarahaua, e, pikipiki ake ra, e,
Ngā moutere tahoratia mai te moana!
Kaore iara, pikipiki ao, pikipiki ao,
Ka puta iara kei tua e!

The sun's rays that shoot up, stretched out,
Climb up over the island, spread out on the sea!
Oh climb up over the world, climb up over the world,
Reach the other side!

T here is something qualitatively different about the way rivers are run and venerated today in New Zealand. I've never seen such a mixing of ritual, reverence, and extreme adventure, an almost mythopoeic approach to what is in some core way an adrenaline ride. I've run rivers around the world—many of them sacred, such as the Ganges, the Indus, the Euphrates, the Yangtze, the Jordan, the Urubamba in the Sacred Valley of the Incas—yet it has been rare to experience such an integrated deference, to witness such a sacramental relationship with the natural environment, and to find water that flows so clean and clear and pure. And I've been involved in helping people around the world learn how to employ wild rivers as eco-attractions for visitors: I trained the Hualapai on the Colorado River, the Batoka along the Zambezi, the Chimbu at the Waghi River of Papua New Guinea. But I've never encountered a local community with such piety for its river. It almost seems religious, though Māori tell me it is something different, a component of an ancient cosmology they call kaitiakitanga.

The concept, one Māori guide tells me, cannot easily be translated, or understood by a Pakeha (someone of European descent, from the Māori word *pakepakeha*, meaning "pale-skinned fairies"), but that hasn't stopped it from becoming a bit of a buzzword throughout New Zealand, with some of its comprehensible elements now being baked into a national ethos. A quiet revolution is taking place down under, a movement to not only preserve what is special and essential about the land but also to improve it, make it better still, for the unborn. The way I interpret it, there is a kind of pay-it-forward sensibility to kaitiakitanga (kye-tee-AH-kee-TAHN-gah), but my grasp seems like a Viking hammer when what is required is a fine, delicate watch tool, and generations of experience, to decorticate the concept's secrets.

Still, whatever the loosely braided ropes of conservation notions behind this philosophy, they were certainly not always predominant, nor was New Zealand a noble arcadia for most of the last thousand years. The first canoe landing was the butterfly that set off a hurricane of ecocide. Before Europeans arrived, Māori deforested more than half the country and hunted several species to extinction. They flunked the Eden test in a pretty impressive way. When I made my first visit to New Zealand

Dale Gardiner blowing up a sandbar on the Kawarau River

in 1978, as a young environmentalist roué, I carried with me one of the first white-water rafts in the country. My friend and fellow river guide Bart Henderson had made the journey the year before and smuggled in what may have been the first such raft. He had made the first descent of the Motu on the North Island the year before and encouraged me to return with him to explore some more waterways.

We flew to Christchurch on the South Island and stayed with one of my heroes, Jon Hamilton, son of Sir William Hamilton, the South Canterbury farmer turned inventor who in 1953 came up with a propellerless river craft to ride up the inches-deep Canterbury rivers. With its shallow draft and high speed, the Hamilton jet boat could nimbly and boldly go where no other boat would dare. In 1960, Jon Hamilton steered his father's water-propelled craft, a boat called *Kiwi,* for nine days up the Colorado

River through the Grand Canyon, negotiating among other obstacles the thirty-five-foot cascade called Lava Falls, the toughest, steepest, and fastest rapid on the Colorado. The expedition, lavishly covered in *National Geographic,* stands as the first and only ascent of the Colorado through the Grand Canyon. Jon went on to make pioneering ascents of the Ganges (with Sir Edmund Hillary), the Yuat of Papua New Guinea (where years later I would make the first descent), and other great rivers around the world. A shard of my mind reminded me that roaring up rivers in metal

Gavin Wills scouting the Tasman River

boats was perhaps not the soundest environmental adventure, but just the same Jon was exploring by water, and in my book he was a river god.

Jon was the perfect host, showing us films of his exotic exploits until the wee hours. The day following, he steered us to meet his nephew, Gavin Wills. Gavin had founded one of the first adventure companies in the country, Alpine Guides, based at Mount Cook, highest and most famous peak in Australasia. Another longtime friend and rafting guide, John Kramer, joined us, and together we unrolled the neoprene white-water raft on the dirt. Gavin poked it as though it were a vehicle from outer space. I showed him how it could host adventure clients for a new facet of his business, and he said, "Let's give it go."

A short time later we were at the headwaters of the Tasman River, which drains the eastern flank of Mount Cook in a wide, braided stream, gray and buzzing with glacial silt. Along with Gavin's adorable, blonde-filamented daughter, Lucy, we piled into the inflatable and bounced and spun down the Tasman to Lake Pukaki, the first such ride ever made on that river and one that would launch a thousand rafts on the South Island. Lucy squealed with delight at this new adventure, reminding me that the joy of rafting is a sanctioned return to childhood, as we adults squealed alongside with every splash, thump, and bob. For years I kept a photo of Lucy on my shelf, poised with a paddle and a grin that would melt glaciers. She went on to become one of New Zealand's top adventurers, until her life was cut shockingly short in 2004 when, at the age of twenty-eight, she succumbed to cancer.

A couple of years later, companies were sprouting to service the new recreation, white-water rafting. A host of rivers were being offered throughout the Southern Alps, a range larger than the Austrian, French, and Swiss Alps combined, with nineteen snowcapped peaks more than ten thousand feet high. The high rainfall (the west side of the Alps receives about half an inch a day) and steep terrain conspire to spill some of the best white water in the world, and rivers such as the Shotover, Kawarau, and Landsborough were becoming legendary in the global river community.

In 1980 I was invited to Queenstown, on the South Island, to present a slide show on the still somewhat novel concept of adventure travel to a group of travel professionals, and I was contacted by a young entrepreneur named Dale Gardiner, who had founded a company called Dane's Back Country. He telexed me at my office in Angels Camp, California, and asked if I might bring over a couple of inflatable rafts, which were still difficult to secure Down Under. I packed a couple of boats in my duffle, forgot to declare them at Customs and Immigration, and handed them over to Dale in Queenstown.

Then he invited me on his own little adventure. We drove to a point in the Kawarau River where a sandbar had encroached far enough into the water to prevent a smooth passage by raft. Dale had decided to do something about it: he had rigged the sandbar with dynamite. I stood on the bank as he blasted away, sending sediment like spiders into the sky and altering the natural design of the river to meet his own vision (and improve business).

I was fascinated and repelled by the exercise, but I felt gritty, like a desert highway after a sandstorm. Some rafters in Arizona had tried the same trick a few months earlier, but were promptly arrested and tossed into jail. I asked the Kiwi outfitter how he could get away with something like this, and he just shrugged: "No worries. It's New Zealand. Anything goes."

I had lived and worked through an era when the Colorado River through the Grand Canyon moved from an unregulated mess to a model of enlightened policies for rafters. In the late 1960s, when I first became a guide, anyone could hurl himself down the river, burn as much wood as he wanted, and shit behind any rock. By the early 1970s, the Colorado had become a stink-hole. Every beach was littered with black ash. Behind every tree were piles of human excrement, and flies had discovered utopia and blackened the banks. When the National Park Service finally stepped in and put in place rules that all waste had to be carried out, the Colorado River beaches actually renewed themselves. Within a couple of years, they were as pristine as when John Wesley Powell passed through in 1869.

The incident on the Kawarau left me with the impression that New Zealand was a place where environmental integrity took a backseat to thrills and commercial interests. When, a few days later, I stood on the banks of the Shotover and held my ears as jet boats screamed by, I concluded that New Zealand was on a downward trajectory when it came to environmental sensitivities and perhaps even wilderness preservation.

That perception began to change with subsequent trips to New Zealand. In 1992 I made a winter visit to Mount Cook, and the whole region seemed brighter and more immaculate than it had a dozen years before. Peradventure it was the winter gloss, I guessed. But then in 2000 I came once again, this time to kayak in the Queen Charlotte Sound. I paddled to Motuara Island, a predator-free wildlife sanctuary, where I saw the rare South Island saddleback, a bird that had once been on the brink of extinction but was reflourishing on this protected isle. At the same time in the States, coastal shelves and Alaska wild lands were being opened to oil exploration. A popular bumper sticker in some parts read, "Save Alaska. Kill a Sierra Clubber," and loggers in the Northwest were offering recipes for roasting or frying the northern spotted owl.

For hundreds of years, it was speculated that somewhere in the Southern Ocean there must be a grand continent to counterbalance the great landmasses of the Northern Hemisphere. Even the mathematician Pythagoras theorized it. Instead, explorers found only Australia and tiny New Zealand. But now, in some way, it seemed there was a shift in balance, not of landmass, but of consciousness and mental infrastructure.

My dash down the Kaituna River with the Māori-owned company named after a hoary concept of environmental stewardship—this thing called kaitiakitanga—reset my own regard for the land here and the people attending to it. I wondered why, over the years, New Zealand remained the one place that seemed to improve with each visit. While in the same frame

I had seen so many special places around the world compromised or lost to commercial exploitation, deforestation, damming, desertification, pollution, or just plain abuse, New Zealand seemed to be improving its lot by taking extra-special care of its wilderness. Prime Minister Helen Clark had even proposed that New Zealand become the first carbon-neutral country in the world, achieving that status by 2020. In a February 2007 speech, she said, "I believe we can aspire to be carbon neutral in our economy and way of life. I believe that in the years to come, the pride we take in our quest for sustainability and carbon neutrality will define our nation, just as our quest for a nuclear-free world has over the past twenty-three years." In other speeches and interviews over the past several years, the prime minister and many others in power have cited the concept of kaitiakitanga as part of the national warp and weft, essential for the custody of the county's future.

So just what is this elusive and crushable exotic bloom called kaitiakitanga, and why is it important here and now?

First descent of the Tasman River, running off the flanks of Mount Cook

SCOTCH ON THE ROCKS

E mua, ata haere; e muri whatiwhati waewae.

The early starters go calmly; those behind will break limbs.

The Māori guides from Kaitiaki Adventures vanish up the trail before I can ask them; they are off to make another run down the Kaituna. So, back at the hotel, I call my friend in Los Angeles, Vanessa Mutu, née Reid. She is a Pakeha, a New Zealander of European descent, but recently married a Māori in a ceremony more successful than an early attempt at such a bicultural union. In 1830 one of the first European settlers was exchanging vows with a Māori girl when an enemy tribe launched a surprise attack and ate the wedding guests. New Zealand is mostly color-blind today, and traditions on all sides are generally honored. Vanessa knows more than anyone else in my circles about Māori beliefs and traditions, and she is swift with counsel.

"Go see my friend John Panoho in Auckland," she says. "He's a Māori elder who founded a company that connects visitors with Māori culture. He can help you."

John agrees to meet me on the beach at Mill Bay, named for the chop shop that once processed native trees not far from his home in the tony neighborhood of Titirangi. He had spent twenty years on the New Zealand Police Force, where he witnessed a surplus of inequities of all stripes. When he retired, he figured he could do something proactive rather than reactive in his next career. In 2003, he and two partners started Navigator Tours, named for his fascination with his forebears' early sea voyages and in tribute to his famous uncle, Hector Busby, the master carver who fashioned the first double-hulled Māori sea canoe in four hundred years. John's business plan is nothing less than to redefine cultural tourism in New Zealand. Tourism is the country's biggest earner of foreign exchange, generating more than 9 percent of the gross domestic product and bringing in more than eight billion New Zealand dollars a year, but as yet John's type of tourism doesn't really register.

Speaking as much with his serene, grandfatherly eyes as with his voice, John says his concept is to conduct a form of tourism that is the "antithesis of Māori entertainment tourism, which has been packaged and presented to visitors for well over one hundred years. It doesn't allow visitors to have any real engagement with our people. It dumbs our culture down."

I listen to John, his professorial white hair flying in the sea breeze, while a colony of barnacles crowds the underside of my memory. I had many times paused at trade shows, poolsides, and hotel lobbies and watched, from a safe distance, various ethnic spectacles and performances, almost choking on the Post-it Note mysticism. I couldn't help but feel that deep, rich cultures and traditions were too often reduced to dinner shows for the mobile rich, après-menu items owned by food-and-beverage managers. In these brief, one-sided encounters, there is no chance to understand the people behind the dances and battle cries, no real celebration of a vibrant, living culture. Visitors are offered the bread crumbs on the floor beneath the big table of cultural apperception.

John is attempting to gather forces of change with a "radical rethink," a set of tours that allow visitors to immerse themselves in the Māori way of life, to get under its skin by working, playing, eating, and experiencing New Zealand with Māori. "The opportunity here is to share what we think, what we believe, to invite others to know a little of our worldview and our relationship with the environment." It all seems not so much brilliant as inevitable.

And it is my opening.

"So, John, knowing that Māori have a relationship with the

View from the Whare Kea Chalet, the only luxury high-mountain hut in New Zealand and one of the few of its caliber in the world

environment that may be something different than that of other peoples of the world, can you explain to me this Māori concept called kaitiakitanga?"

John knits his eyebrows and seems to consider his words before speaking. "You're delving into a spiritual realm here, into a concept that some believe Pakeha can never really comprehend. But I can give you a few pointers:

"First, you have to travel with an open mind.

"Second, you have to know that to Māori, everything has a spirit. You may see someone talking to his carved walking stick, but that is because it is imbued with its own spirit, just as each rock, tree, fish, star, whale, dolphin, river, and mountain.

"Third, notice that when a Māori takes shellfish from the sea, he takes enough for his family, but no more.

23

"Fourth, every element of the natural world has a minder, a guide—a kaitiaki. The kaitiaki honor what they are charged to keep, and you in turn must honor and respect the kaitiaki.

"And finally, at least for now, if you travel this country, from the bottom to the top, and spend time and talk to and connect with people from all walks of life, Māori and Pakeha alike, and follow the shadow of the *kotuku,* the white herons who carry the spirits of kaitiaki to the far north, to the spirit tree that hangs over the point where two oceans meet, then—perhaps then—you will begin to have a sense of an understanding of kaitiakitanga."

So it is I set out to voyage to a concept beyond my reach, like Captain Willard traveling upriver seeking Colonel Kurtz. I am on a quest to travel the length of New Zealand to see if I might find the phantom behind the spray of kaitiakitanga, and perhaps a key to knowing why the people of this isolated land are seemingly so environmentally alert and shrewd. And to dig down a bit to know if this concept is in some way a chimera, a marketing ploy, political preening, or greenwashing. When it comes to the rhetoric surrounding "green" these days, you could comfortably drive a Hummer through the gap between most words and most deeds. The new yellow journalism is green. Or

Queenstown, the adventure hub of the Pacific

24

is this something different, something with depth and resonance, something perhaps quite important? This I hope to find out, and so I book a flight to the south of the South Island of New Zealand.

I had bumped around Queenstown, the adventure hub of the Pacific, on previous visits, so I decide to begin this little expedition in the nearby town of Wanaka, which is where Tom Peirce's family owned a home and which Tom, who traveled globally for a living, often called out as exceptional. The town curves around Lake Wanaka at the edge of Mount Aspiring National Park, one of fourteen national parks in New Zealand, all free to all visitors. Together with reserves and other conservation-status areas, they cover more than a third of the country.

Here, at a fish-and-chips takeout, I meet Ian Murray, a fifth-generation Kiwi of Irish heritage with a shot of Scotch and self-appointed Māori membership. He speaks fluent Te Reo Māori, knows the stories, and has adopted the Māori magico-religious worldview as his own. He calls himself a "white Māori," sports two Māori *mokos* (tattoos), and around his neck wears a *koru* pendant. The shape, he tells me, is a Māori symbol of creation, based on the contour of an unfurling fern frond. The circular form conveys the idea of perpetual movement, and its inward coil suggests a return to the point of origin, symbolizing the way life changes and stays the same. I assume that if any non-Māori knows the meaning of kaitiakitanga, it must be Ian. But when asked, he shrugs and says he is not a tall poppy—not someone who pretends to know more than others in this famously egalitarian society. "It's not in the dictionary. Academics try to screw it down, but they can't. I can't. But I can take you to people who know," he volunteers.

Ian is by any measure a difficult man not to like. It turns out we are antipodean doppelgangers, to a degree: we are the same ripe age, and we each started guiding at nineteen, he taking tourists on jet boats up the rapids of the South Island and I taking guests on rafts down the Colorado through the Grand Canyon. We both labored diligently in the vineyards of adventure travel for the best part of our careers. He witnessed front row the trends, the dips, the experiments, and reached the conclusion that New Zealand is simply not a resort destination nor designed for a tourist culture of "massclusivity." Its assets are its Mesozoic beauty, its vegetative exuberance, its spate of adventures, and its rich culture. As we tool about town, he fills me in on some history.

New Zealand, it is theorized, was once part of the southern super-continent Gondwanaland, which included Antarctica, South America, Africa, Australia, New Guinea, Arabia, the Indian subcontinent, and New Zealand. (The name is from the Gondwana region of central northern India, which in turn derives its name from the Sanskrit *gondavana,* meaning "forest of Gond.") The continent began to dismember during the mid-Jurassic, and New Zealand began to sail away on its solo mission about one hundred million years ago. It is natural and tempting to compare a place to others seen, but that doesn't work here. New Zealand evolved so that some 85 percent of its flora and avifauna are endemic—unique and sometimes bizarre species in a lost world.

New Zealand was the last major landmass settled by humans—people who traveled thousands of miles across the Pacific in stout canoes following the morning sun. They hailed from an empyrean realm called Hawaiki, the place of the ancients and the gods, somewhere in eastern Polynesia, perhaps the Cook Islands. In between there and here was the huge, seamless marine continent called "Te Moana Nui a Kiwa," "the great ocean of Kiwa."

As do all explorers, they created myths to help explain a mystifying new world, ensuring that what was around them would fortify the truths within them. The stories (the word derives from the Latin *historia,* meaning "history") were purposeful constructs created to condense the structure of the world into easily graspable forms. Those first settlers believed the two main islands of New Zealand were created by the demigod Maui-tikitiki-a-Taranga, or Maui for short. As a boy, Maui learned he had magic powers, but he kept them to himself. One day he wanted to go fishing with his older brothers, but they didn't want his company. So Maui hid under the floorboards of their canoe, or *waka,* climbing out only when they were far out to sea. His brothers were righteously upset, but rather than return, they went fishing.

Maui pulled out his own hook, made from a fragment of their grandmother's jawbone, but his older brothers wouldn't share the bait. So he struck his nose and smeared the hook with his own blood. He then dropped the hook into the water, and, BAM, he hooked a big one. Reciting a magical chant that made heavy things light, he slowly hauled the fish to the surface.

When the fishermen saw the immense size of the catch, Maui said the gods must be angry and asked his brothers to wait while he returned to Hawaiki and appealed to the higher powers. But his brothers wouldn't listen and leapt from the waka to scale the big fish. The leviathan raised its fins and writhed in agony. At that instant the sun rose, turning the fish from flesh into a rough and mountainous land, which the brothers named "Te-Ika-a-Maui," "the fish of Maui."

It's true that from a satellite the North Island resembles a fish, specifically a stingray. The southern tip near Wellington is the head of the fish, with its harbor the mouth, and the northern tip is the tail, though how the ancient Māori could have imagined this overhead view is a bit of a mystery. The South Island is said to be Maui's overturned waka, with the Southern Alps forming the keel of the canoe. I don't have to squint to see this rugged land as the backbone of an overturned canoe. Tiny Stewart Island, to the south, is viewed as the anchor of the great canoe. The storytelling makes the metaphysical stirrings not only plausible but also irresistible to even the rational scoffer.

"A tool of the gods"—that's how Māori viewed Mount Aspiring, a stunning peak in the Southern Alps with pyramid contours reminiscent of the Matterhorn. Māori call it Tititea, or "glittering peak." According to lore, a demiurge used this peak as a tool to gouge out the coastal fjords of the South Island. Now it sits, upended and abandoned, calling for company.

In much of the alpine world, a mountain this rhapsodic would be riddled with roads, tunnels, trains, and *téléphériques,* but Mount Aspiring soars alone amid a vast, protected park with practically no accoutrements of civilization. There is a notable exception, though: a new eco-lodge that sits on a high shoulder in the Buchanan Mountains across the valley from Mount Aspiring. But guests don't check in the usual way: they fly in by helicopter.

Ian drives me up Mount Aspiring Road, an apt name considering the size of its ruts. At first the road shows a definite purpose. But after a time its good intentions fade, and it reverts to its antediluvian origins, strolling along cheerful and inconsequential like a shepherd boy out with a flock of unruly sheep. Everywhere stand trees in companies, tall, slender, russet-leaved, with delicate canopies of twigs—lacy umbrellas. Whatever principles of sustainability are applied here seem to be working. Now that we've traveled a few bends together, I turn and again ask Ian what he knows of kaitiakitanga.

"Well, kaitiakitanga is a value, you know. It is a responsibility. It is a feeling, an emotion. It's hard to put that into words. When Māori talk to Māori and the word *kaitiakitanga* is mentioned, they don't transfer it into an English meaning because I don't know really if you can capture the essence. I don't know if there's an English equivalent or a translation of the meaning. So the catchphrase is 'guardianship,' but I know it's a whole lot more."

In the robed light of the afternoon, we pull into a cattle, sheep, and deer station alongside Lake Wanaka. Ian deposits me in front of a Hughes 500 E helicopter with a door detached on the passenger side. Already feeling a bit chilly here at the base, I dig into my duffel and layer myself with as many sweaters and jackets as I can find. As I squeeze into the helicopter, pilot Alex Ewing, in shorts and a T-shirt, shoots me the same look the man at the car wash gives an RV wheeling into line. But Alex gamely flies me, sans Ian, up the glaciated Matukituki Valley, which appears to have not a smudge of nonwilderness. In such immensity, the tiny chopper feels inconsequential, like a blown feather. Twenty minutes later, at a windy shelf more than a mile high, we land by a modern-looking wood-and-glass shelter called the Whare Kea Chalet, the only luxury high-mountain hut in New Zealand and one of the few of its caliber in the world.

I step out of the bird. The air is cool and expectant, and the panorama is more cinematic than real. We can scan what seems the entire alpine world, rolling and whispering and calling.

UNCOMMON CURRENCY

Kia ū ki te mana, ihi, wehi, o ngā mea katoa.

Hold strong the sacredness, prestige, and awe of all things created.

Paul Aubrey, the chief guide for Adventure Consultants, has joined this outing. He gives me a tour of the room at the top, pointing out that New Zealand had eco-lodges long before the term existed. The mountain hut system along the tracks of New Zealand is among the world's best. The huts were designed with simplicity and sustainability in mind long before any architectural trend.

Built in the mid-1990s by Martyn Myer of the Melbourne retailing family, the chalet has all the modern eco-facets: solar panels and a wind turbine, roof-collected water, a policy of carrying out all waste (by helicopter), and that most important accessory, an Italian espresso machine. And it has a room with a view, through long glass panels that overlook the sweep of the Southern Alps, a glimpse of the lopsided northeast face of Mount Aspiring, and the outcrop imaginatively called the Pope's Nose.

Helicopters are not the quietest or cleanest way into the unavailing wilderness. But New Zealand is mountainous, rugged, and remote. And

New Zealand had eco-lodges long before the term existed.

New Zealand ferries more people into its back-country by helicopter than any other country in the world. Some argue that this mode of transport is inconsistent with the spirit of wilderness stewardship. Just in terms of greenhouse gases, a

Inside the Whare Kea Chalet Built in the mid-1990s, the chalet has all the modern eco-facets.

forty-five-minute helicopter ride emits about three hundred fifty pounds of carbon dioxide. But consider this: the more people who travel to the wilderness and are touched by its beauty, spirit, and magic—the more people who become emotionally connected with a place—the larger the constituency of those who will contribute voices, energy, time, and treasure when the place becomes threatened, as it always does. The unlit places of hearts and minds are the ones that go up in smoke.

Paul Aubrey guides people into the wilderness for a living and believes, as I do, that showcasing these special places is the motor to saving them. As a mountain guide, his currency is unmediated wilderness, and thus he has an economic as well as a spiritual motivation to be an active steward. I ask if he knows the concept of kaitiakitanga, and he looks at me blankly, almost as though I'm treading into a Kiwi version of *omertà*, the code of silence that keeps Mafiosi from ratting. After a few beats, he replies that he has heard of it, doesn't really understand it, but thinks he is practicing it. Because the impulse still seems to me like a remote landscape only really known to birds of passage, I have to agree.

Back in Wanaka, we drive by a life-size model of a moa, the giant, flightless bird that once tramped around New Zealand in great numbers, but which was extirpated by early Māori settlers. Because there were no ground mammals, Māori hunted moa for protein (a drumstick was the size of a leg of beef); for the bones, which made excellent fishhooks and ornaments; and for the feathers, which were used for frocks. All eleven species of moa disappeared by about AD 1500, as did about a dozen other species of birds, including an eagle, a crow, a pelican, a harrier hawk, swans, geese, ducks, and rails. This period may have seen the most devastating and rapid loss of bird species in the history of the planet. Māori used fire to flush prey from the forests, destroying both in the process. The first Europeans to arrive saw the plains as a desert, tussocky and gravelly, often lacking freshwater. Extolling Māori as environmental exemplars sometimes seems a bit like putting a cat on the cover of *Mouse Magazine,* but their history may be just an example of failing wisely. Early Māori no doubt believed, as many of us do today about resources such as clean water, minerals, and oil, that the supply was eternal. The two main islands of New Zealand were the largest that Polynesian seafarers

The author and Kylie Ruwhiu-Karawana at Lake Wanaka

had ever encountered. Together they make up almost 90 percent of Polynesian land. They were more physically and climatically diverse than the coral atolls and basalt islands from which the Polynesians came. To the colonizers, the forests, minerals, and birdlife must have seemed never-ending.

In town I meet Kylie Ruwhiu-Karawana, one of the new generation of Māori involved in tourism and a keen exegete for her culture. We walk along the rocky beach of Lake Wanaka, and I ask her about Māori connectedness to the land upon which we are stepping.

"We are the land and the land is us," she says as a preface to a story reminiscent of Mesopotamian theology. "Our primordial mother is Papatua-nuku, Mother Earth; our primordial father is Ranginui, the sky. When the god children of both parents divided up between themselves

The author in Mount Aspiring National Park: "A tool of the gods"—that's how Māori viewed Mount Aspiring, a stunning peak in the Southern Alps with pyramid contours reminiscent of the Matterhorn. Māori call it Tititea, or "glittering peak."

the various kingdoms of the earth, Lord Tangaroa took the sea, and Lord Tāne, the father of man, took the forests and its lands. This forged the close kinship of man and with the residents of the sea.

"Whenever we introduce ourselves," Kylie says, "you'll notice it's all about where we come from. The last thing we say is our name—because the rivers and mountains are our people."

The sun scatters its spokes across the water of the lake. A breeze sails past, negligible as a faint breath. I pick up a flat stone and skip it across the water. It seems to blur the reflections of the trees—trees that don't naturally belong here—shaking the seeming solid surface of reality.

"When you look around, you see a beautiful lake and stunning mountains and perhaps the beautiful rivers that feed this beautiful lake," Kylie continues. "But I see a tapestry of stories that bring the landscape to life. I don't see a mountain. I see a chapter in a book. A mountain is a warrior who has fought many battles; the river, a compliant woman. The lake is a playfield of giants. The gods would gouge out the earth with a mighty *kō* [digging stick] and wait for the water to fill, and play in the puddles, just as kids do today."

Kylie's metaphysics is far removed from that of much of the world. On the one side are those who believe that scientific observation of the universe leaves no room for the supranatural—that the world conforms to strict mechanical laws in an absolutely predictable manner. On the other side is the conviction that man is separate from nature and should seek dominion over it, as God designed. It was only recently that Pope Benedict XVI made clear his belief that man has a unique, God-given role that is above all else, living or otherwise. "Man is the only creature on earth that God willed for his own sake," says a document issued under Pope John Paul II and approved by then–Cardinal Ratzinger, now Pope Benedict. This element of faith is not unique to Catholicism or Christianity. The inanimate do not have spirits in most of the world's religions. Māori, however, have no words to distinguish science from religion, scholarship from belief. Theirs is a betwixt worldview, the third point of a classic Hegelian dialectical triangle, a subtle third way that draws on the tensions and contradictory natures of the other two. It could be, I imagine, the realization of Hegel's declaration of humanity's most advanced thought, the idea that recognizes itself in all things.

But now as I look around, no matter how hard I blink or squint, all I see are rock and a fathomless lake.

"That's normal," Kylie says. "If you spend enough time on Aotearoa ["land of the long white cloud," the Māori name for New Zealand, which is finding new currency today], you will hear our stories, proverbs, and songs, and you will come to know that this land has a heart, a soul, and you will start to see through our eyes and through the eyes of Maui."

Kaitiakitanga seems a cloudlike notion. My eyes notice that Kylie is wearing a smooth, curved, jadelike carving around her neck, and I ask its significance.

"It's a *taonga,* a treasure, made from greenstone from a river near here, charged with the spiritual energy of my ancestors. We call the stone *pounamu,* and we call the South Island Te Wai Pounamu, meaning 'the land of the greenstone water.'"

I had read a bit about taonga in the Auckland museum. A taonga can be any object that represents the identity of a Māori kin group with its land and resources. Taonga can be tangible, such as a cloak, a greenstone weapon, or a war canoe, or intangible, such as the knowledge to carve, to recite genealogy, or to sing a lament. As taonga are passed down through the generations, they become more valuable as the number of descendants increases. Taonga are the divine personifications of particular ancestors. Thus they are time travelers, bridging generations, allowing descendants to meet their ancestors ritually, face to face.

According to lore, a demiurge used Mount Aspiring as a tool to gouge out the coastal fjords of the South Island. Now it sits upended and abandoned, calling for company.

Kylie holds her taonga to the sun, and I see its inner lines rise and flare like the bloom of a calla lily. She tells me she never takes it off except to shower, and then she reaches into her bag and retrieves what looks like a stone fishhook attached to a string necklace. She drapes it over my neck. "This is your taonga. It has healing powers. It speaks to your heart and makes you feel safe and warm and comfortable on the inside. And if you travel with it, it might help you connect with our land and our people and understand where we are coming from."

There seems ingenuity in Kylie's narrative, which passes back and forth between animate and inanimate with such structural assurance and isometric tightness that the continuity is undisturbed.

It is, I find, energizing to spend time with someone so spirited and spiritual, so embracing of a culture that not long ago came close to capsizing. But Kylie has one more surprise. As we stop on the beach and Kylie gazes with her fox eyes at the range that indeed could be the keel of a great overturned canoe, she breaks out into a Māori song with a voice so spotless, so divinely beautiful, that it would appear no further argument for the numinous élan of Māori need ever be proffered.

> *Hutia te rito*
> *Hutia te rito o te harakeke*
> *Kei hea te komako e ko*
> *He aha te mea nui I te ao*
> *Maku e ki atu e*
> *He tangata he tangata*
> *He tangata hei.*

She translates the chorus: "If you remove the center of the flax bush, where will the bellbird sing? What is the most important thing in the world? I would reply: it is people, it is people, it is people." It is shards of cosmic grace stressed into singular things—an apologue, perhaps, for the whole of the planet.

"Listen and learn what you can here, and after a while the landscape may for you become a person," Kylie says. "And when you go home, when you look at the mountains, rivers, and lakes in your country, hopefully they will take on personas, and you will want to become a kaitiaki for your own home."

LESS BAD
IS GOOD

Kia tapu te mara o Papatuanuku. He karakia mo tera mara mo tika kai me mahi kai.

Keep the garden of mother earth sacred and open through appropriate incantations for all things and when planting or gathering food.

T hat night I settle in at a quaint inn nestled among the lakeside willows and golden poplars.

While much of the scenic world has allowed resort development that ravages the land, shatters traditional culture, and spirits money to overseas concerns, New Zealand has been a captain and an exemplar in embracing eco-friendly lodgings. Wanaka Homestead is one of many. It succeeds in living the oxymoron of being both sumptuous and environmentally sound, blending traditional architecture and materials with modern conveniences and comfort. It consumes half the energy typical for this type of luxury accommodation. Builders used recycled timber from farm sheds and extra insulation to keep heat from escaping. They employed solar power to heat water and trap radiation in a large, under-floor heating system. Even the hot tub is part of the solar hot-water system. Electrical devices are either low-energy or controlled by timers. In 2004, Wanaka Homestead won a "Highly Commended" Energywise Award in the renewable-energy category from New Zealand's Energy Efficiency and Conservation Authority, and it has been a member of Green Globe 21 for several years. It generates an estimated fifty fewer tons of carbon dioxide per year than a similar conventional lodging.

John Panoho had told me that Māori think in terms of community while Pakeha think in terms of the individual. In that regard, Wanaka Homestead has a Māori sensibility. It supports community initiatives, events, and groups through some NZ$10,000 per year of sponsorships. Founder Roger North, a former civil engineer, is an actively involved trustee of Sustainable Wanaka, an organization that seeks to help others help themselves.

I am thrilled to see a concept realized this extensively. I know too well from my travels that resort tourists too often see what cannot naturally occur: an idyllic, insulated retreat with all the amenities of a Beverly Hills hotel. For these deep-pocketed visitors, trees are felled, swamps drained, rivers dammed, and villages shoved aside to preserve the "natural feel" of a contrived paradise. Even more sadly, the villagers may find their traditional livelihoods as fishers, farmers, and artisans supplanted by a resort economy built around touro-dollars, leaving them to find work only in the white-smocked service and support industries, learning new words for new skills and new vices. The result of this type of tourism is all too often pollution, both environmental and cultural, and the damage is too frequently irrevocable.

The prefix "eco-" has been stretched and bled and mangled and manipulated as a marketing tool, so it's important that conscientious travelers ask the right questions when it comes to accommodations. Is the lodge environmentally sound? It is energy efficient? Does it employ local talent? Does it use local materials? And, ultimately, where does the money go? If there is no local economic benefit, then it will fail.

So I request a tour from Roger and ask right up, is his creation an "eco-lodge"?

"No," he bolts from the blue. "I call this a 'less-bad lodge.'" He explains that to him, "eco" implies a purity that can't be reached but can be aspired to. He has aimed to craft a lodge that honors the more natural actualizations of yurts, mud huts, and tepees, but has none of the disadvantages of yesteryear. As we stroll around what looks like a classic alpine lodge, he points out the apotropaic devices he has employed: The largest double-glazed windows face north (we are, of course, in the Southern

At the heart of the southern lakes is Lake Wanaka, gateway to Mount Aspiring National Park and host to the Wanaka Homestead.

Hemisphere), passively catching light and heat as sails catch wind. On the opposite side, the southern exposures, there are no windows, and the solid schist-and-mudstone walls keep heat in. Inside the toasty parlor, he pulls back the lamp coverings to show the romantically named 827 low-energy fluorescent lights, which give off a nice yellow glow. He points out the eight solar panels on the roof, manufactured in China, perhaps the least environmentally minded place on earth, and he admits he loses points for this outsourcing, but the product is good and well-priced. His venture is a business, after all. "We borrowed money to build this, and the money we save on power bills exceeds the loan repayments. It's a no-brainer. It's what sustainability is all about."

Indeed, the place is a far cry from the prefabs the original English settlers shipped from the homeland. It is appointed with natural wood furniture and locally crafted art and evokes a high-end aesthetic in every detail, and yet running it costs less than half of what a typical lodge of similar size would require. Roger passes the savings on to guests. It costs less, and he makes more.

Roger's thinking and execution seem so aligned with what I have heard of Māori sensibility I have to pop the question:

"Have you heard of kaitiakitanga, and if so, does this effort fit into the concept?"

"Yes," he says, "I know a bit of the concept, and I think it's a wonderful, wonderful thing. This lodge expresses it, I believe. It's something holistic. It's about planning for the future, I think, and Māori have a long tradition of honoring that, including in their own buildings. I think it just proves Māori were ahead of the game before we were.

"I was very much a mainstream person into my twenties, and then gradually I became more environmentally aware. By the time I was thirty, I was pretty much depressed, not quite clinically, but really in quite a bad mental state from lack of solutions and wondering where mankind was going and really not feeling good about it. So part of my solution was this whole business of thinking globally and acting locally, where what we can really do is to change things in your own life that can make a difference. So when we got the opportunity to build something new, it was a logical time to apply that, so that I could be true to these principles.

"Now I have never been so happy in my own life. To me the principle of kaitiakitanga pretty much says, in a single word, exactly how I feel about the whole Roger North. I'm still not too happy about the way the whole world is going, but let's put it this way: this is a commercial business, and the energy savings we've made on this are at least half of what's normal. If people applied these energy savings in their own homes, where there is a wider choice of how to behave—making choices such as being comfortable in a slightly cooler environment, being more sensible about turning off appliances—I'm quite sure that energy consumption could be reduced by 80 percent without affecting quality of life. It's just mainstream normal living with a little bit of thought behind it.

"It drives me nuts that most of the world continues to invent ways to generate more instead of ways to consume less. To me, kaitiakitanga is the way forward."

Sustainability was certainly an alien concept to the original European settlers in New Zealand. The unstated common objective was to siphon off the assets of the territory, including seals, whales, timber, and gold. The myth of unlimited wealth in the Pacific became so deeply embedded in Western consciousness and entwined in Victorian notions of progress that it is still a huge challenge to change.

Perhaps it goes deeper than that. Consider the government tourist offices between World Wars I and II, whose brochures and magazine advertisements attempted to lure world-cruise travelers to the paradisiacal Southern Alps. The Edenic myth is deeply implanted in Western tradition, with roots in both classic and biblical soil. It was kept alive in the Middle Ages by cartographers, who customarily showed the antediluvian Promised Land as being in the southern Pacific. The romancers of the Age of Discovery had little difficulty in placing Elysium in the exotic lands that curl Down Under, which they would people variously with noble savages, lost tribes, or superior human beings. The early European explorers, both globetrotters and narrators, gave open support to this kind of thinking—the British naval captain James Cook among them. This mind-set persists today in the expectations of many tourists who come here blatantly searching for the green mansions of paradise—but a paradise brought poolside, without any requisite to connect or understand.

TART
IMITATING
LIFE

He toa rere moana he kai tēna mā te wai.

A daring sailor shall become food for the waves.

After I enjoy a rhapsodic and guilt-free night's sleep in the Wanaka Homestead, Ian wants to take me north, to the glaciers that kiss the Tasman Sea.

We wend our way up over the Haast Pass along State Highway 6, the southernmost road crossing of the Southern Alps. The namesake is Sir Johann Franz Julius von Haast, a German geologist who went looking for gold and was among the first Europeans to make the crossing in the 1860s. Māori, of course, had traveled this route for some time before Europeans, in search of food and greenstone, but made no fuss over naming or improving.

By 1876, prospectors had carved a hard rock path, and by the following year cattle were being driven over the hump. It was another fifty-two years before an attempt was made to turn the pass into a real road, but the effort took a bit longer than expected. The road was finished in 1960, with a link to the Fox Glacier in 1965. And it wasn't until 1995 that it was finally paved. Still, we see no cars or people en route. The noisiest thing on the road is the explosion of wildflowers. New Zealand is one of the world's least-crowded countries, with a density of just 39 people per square mile in a country about two-thirds the size of California. That U.S. state, which has some impressive wilderness tracts, packs 217 people into each square mile.

We skate into Te Wahipounamu, the South West New Zealand World Heritage Area, where we pull over at the edge of the darkling Haast River. Roots and ferns cling like dragon claws to the banks. Here we board a steel-bottomed, enclosed safari jet boat operated by sometime racer Lindsay Kain. With Lindsay at the wheel, we snarl downriver, executing emetic peels around sandbars, Tokyo-drifting the bends, sending spray flying in huge arcs and birds scattering to the sheltering sky. This is giddy stuff, a sort of horizontal roller-coaster sensation; it is impossible to suppress grins and hoots. But this seems a guilty pleasure too, as the noise and fuel it takes to penetrate this glacial valley—a protected area no less—somehow seems not quite in the spirit of kaitiakitanga. Yet I know as well as anyone that in many places, wilderness is an elitist precept,

Sir William Hamilton, the South Canterbury farmer turned inventor, came up with a propellerless river craft to ride up the inches-deep Canterbury rivers.

available only to the fit and able and young. Here in New Zealand, jet boats provide wilderness access for almost anyone of any stripe—any shape, age, or income level. Lindsay promotes his tour as a "close-up encounter with nature at its very best," designed for "the mature traveler in mind." For many of his guests, this is the only way into this wild backcountry, and they, if only for a moment, experience the awe and renewal that only the wilderness transmits. It is an inspired transformation of life into movement.

I witnessed this firsthand many years ago when I was a guide on the Colorado River through the Grand Canyon for Hatch River Expeditions. The founder, Bus Hatch, had conducted some of the first commercial raft trips in the West, starting in his home state of Utah in 1929. After the Korean War, he bought bundles of military-surplus, thirty-three-foot-long, neoprene pontoon bridges, which he fashioned into white-water tour boats by slapping on wooden frames and transoms and hanging twenty-horsepower Mercury outboard engines off the back.

When I began commercial guiding in the late 1960s, I piloted one of these motorized rafts, and my clients skewed to a higher age spectrum than those who signed up to buck downstream in wooden dories or the smaller, inflatable rowing rafts. Once I even guided a group from the Foundation of the Junior Blind down the river and watched in my own wonder as they delighted in rubbing their palms along the polished basalt walls while our raft bobbed in an eddy. Yet, sometimes I was booed when I ground past a quiet campsite lined with the whispering dories, and the blue smoke from the motor oil we used visibly whorled up the cathedral-like canyon in our wakes. We were not eco-friendly in any trenchant sense, but we did showcase the glories of the Grand Canyon to an audience that otherwise would not have found admission. And when plans for dams in "The Ditch," as we guides called our place of work, steamrolled forward, they were blocked and buried by the combined efforts of rafters and ardent conservationists. I'm convinced that if those I guided down the Colorado had been unable to make the passage on motorized rafts, the Grand Canyon, one of the seven natural wonders of the world, would be dammed today.

Back on the highway, the thick, juicy light begins to fold in on itself, and the agonizingly scenic West Coast Road seems to keen and howl with the wind like a road winding into some epic tragedy. The high and bony trees are bent, glabrous on the sea side, woolly and windblown on the other, looking as though they were caught in the action of running away. Rudyard Kipling referred to Auckland as "last, loneliest, loveliest, exquisite, apart," but the words seem to fit this stretch of shore even better.

This is a coast for the centuries. When Abel Tasman sailed along this uncertain edge in December 1642, he was so abashed with what he could see—"a land uplifted high"—that he hightailed north without setting foot ashore, but with impressions that would shape history.

The quest that set Abel Janszoon Tasman sailing had its origins in the late thirteenth century, when Marco Polo reached the China seas and heard of the fabulous province of "Beach" somewhere to the south. Rumors circulated for the next three hundred fifty years that Beach held a biota richer than Europe or America, plump with gold, silver, and spices. Sir Frances Drake sought it to no avail, as did lesser explorers. Finally, in 1642, Tasman was dispatched from the Dutch East Indies (today's Indonesia) for "the discovery and exploration of the supposed rich southern and eastern land."

It was on the west coast of the South Island that Tasman had dropped anchor when, in the thickening dusk, two double-hulled canoes sped out for the first recorded European–Māori encounter.

Whether or not Arthur C. Clarke's Third Law, that "any sufficiently advanced technology is indistinguishable from magic," held true for Māori as they faced the equivalent of a spaceship and dodged shots from magic sticks, it didn't stop them from killing a boatload of Dutchmen ostensibly sent to "make friends." Tasman watched in horror as Māori clubbed to death three of his men, then took the body of a fourth to shore, where he was assumed to have been cooked and eaten, as that was the ritual means of absorbing the spiritual power of a vanquished foe.

Tasman declined to set foot on this uncongenial littoral but did christen it Murderer's Bay, which two hundred years later British settlers renamed Golden Bay, as though they were readying for a tourist invasion. Tasman didn't do well at having names stick. He called the land he sailed alongside Staten Landt, believing it was connected to an island near the southern tip of South America, which another Dutchman, Jacob Le Maire, had discovered and named Staten Landt in 1616. When in 1643 this was determined to be impossible, an anonymous cartographer in the Dutch East India Company renamed Tasman's discovery Niew Zeeland, after the Dutch province.

For the next 126 years, New Zealand sailed quietly in its own private waters. Then, in 1768, Captain James Cook was instructed to seek the legendary southern continent, and in 1769–70 he made the first circumnavigation of New Zealand. After connecting the dots, he wrote that his circling of New Zealand meant "the total demolition of our aeriel fabrick called Continent." He also called the shoreline along which we are now driving "an inhospitable shore."

The next century found Frenchman Jules de Blosseville penning in 1823 that the shoreline was "one long solitude, with forbidding sky and frequent tempest." Not long afterward, French explorer Dumont D'Urville described it in a single word: "Frightful."

Then, from 1846 until mid-1848, the British-born surveyor Thomas Brunner spent 550 days exploring the west coast of the South Island. At one point, he was reduced to a diet of fern root, penguin, rat, and finally his own beloved dog. He summed the place up as "the very worst country I have seen in New Zealand. For what reason the natives choose to live here I cannot imagine."

But Māori appreciated the west coast for its natural bounty, especially the greenstone, and did not find negotiating the land as challenging as did Brunner and his ilk. Charles Heaphy, a soldier on Brunner's ill-fated expedition, wrote of their Māori guide, Ekehu: "Thoroughly acquainted with the bush, [Ekehu] appears to have an instinctive sense far beyond our comprehension. . . . A good shot . . . A capital manager of a canoe, a sure snare of wildfowl and a superb fellow at a ford, he is worth his weight in tobacco."

A faint carnival of stars starts to twinkle as we turn off the tar seal, as they call asphalt here. Our tires crackle down a dirt road in the dark and up to a building blazing with lights—no energy efficiency in evidence here. As we pull up alongside the front porch, we seem to have slipped through a time warp. There to greet us are three women dressed in the tight bodices and puffy skirts of matinee-movie Wild West saloon girls. We're at the Franz Josef Glacier Country Retreat, a replica of a historical west-coast homestead, newly built on a two-hundred-acre farm by the fourth-generation descendants of gold-mining pioneers. Marie Coburn, the owner, and her two hostesses stay in character and period dress throughout the stay. They entice us into their own reality-distortion field as we pad around hundred-year-old furnishings surrounded by hanging daguerreotypes, sip brandy from snifters, and stuff ourselves with the hearty fare of turn-of-the-twentieth-century frontiersmen. It may not be an eco-lodge, or even a less-bad lodge, but it does carry the tincture of time and honor traditions, which have their own merits.

After a sleep in a brocade-pillowed and red-feathered room and a soak in a clawed tub, I meet Ian in the breakfast room and ask how he's doing. "Box of fluffy ducks," he declares, admitting, I think, that his own sleep had been lightly carbonated.

HELL FREEZES OVER

Whāia e koe te iti kahurangi; ki te tuohu koe,
me maunga teitei.

Seek the treasure you value most dearly; if you bow your head,
let it be to a lofty mountain.

Moving back to the present, we set out to see the fabled Franz Josef Glacier, one of more than three thousand glaciers in New Zealand. As my friend Michael Kaye, the Costa Rica–based "godfather of ecotourism," likes to say when asked about all the marketing spin and green lipstick attached to cosmetic environmental-crisis solutions, "We can't fool glaciers into melting less." Yet the Franz Josef Glacier is world-renowned these days and loved by a certain set of polemics and politicians because it is one of the few glaciers in the world not retreating. Rather, it is galloping forward at a rate of up to a dozen feet a day. It is cold comfort for the climate-change disbelievers, even though glacial ice represents the largest reservoir of freshwater on earth and in most other locales is melting at a terrifying rate.

Down at Franz Josef Township, I'm led to a small airfield, and minutes later I am soaring over the iris-blue ice of Westland National Park in a buffeting helicopter along with Craig Butland, glacier manager for Franz Josef Glacier Guides. Just below what looks like a tsunami frozen midwave, we land, to an icy reception. The glacier is groaning. We're at about two thousand three hundred feet above sea level on a moving river of ice. I attach crampons, grab an ice ax, and start to crunch through this netherworld, first explored in 1865 by Julius von Haast, who named it after the Austrian emperor of the day.

There is a reason such a great body of literature centers on mountains and glaciers. To traverse these landscapes is to be a part of a narrative rich with risk, conflict, and perhaps understanding. Here one can test one's fire against the flying ice and be a part of a moving myth.

The lusty nature of the Franz Josef Glacier is due in good part to the west coast's abundance of rain-drenched winds from the west. The precipitation falls as snow high up in the névés, which then crystallizes to form clear ice that runs as a frozen river. This and the adjacent Fox Glacier constitute the only glacier system at this latitude, forty-three degrees south, that has advanced so close to the sea. It is certainly among the few glacier systems rimmed in rain forest and ferns.

I step into an electric blue maze. Why is it so blue? It is the effect known as Rayleigh scattering, named after Lord Rayleigh, the Nobel Prize–winning English physicist who codiscovered the element argon. It has something to do with minute air bubbles contained in the solid ice, which scatter blue light better than they do other colors in the light spectrum. The harder the ice, the bluer it appears.

I can hear the sound of melted ice rushing through honeycombed caverns beneath my boots. Slowly, gingerly, I track over crevasses and around sinkholes, kettle lakes, and towers of fractured ice. Making my way over billowing, serrated expanses, listening to streams tumbling underfoot like rolling, empty oil drums, I explore the glacier, ducking into ice caves, tiptoeing along shimmering edges. I stoop into a sapphire grotto, what geologists call a *moulin,* where a slip could leave a body swallowed by the gash, which might then abruptly close with the shifting ice, grinding the victim to powder. The mutability of water, which switches between liquid and solid states more quickly and frequently than any other matter on the planet, helps make the erosive quality of glaciers enormous. All around is the evidence.

After a few hours of picking through this crucible of ice—with its fluted temples, eroded pinnacles, tunnels, pools, battlements, and frozen surf—the weather rolling in from the Tasman Sea appears to be "about to spit the dummy," as Ian says, so the helicopter makes a pickup to ferry us

The Franz Josef Glacier is world-renowned these days because it is one of the few glaciers in the world that is not retreating.

back to terra firma. The clouds have turned as purple as a bruise, and the air smells of rain, but before heading down-ice, the pilot swoops the helicopter upward, up the prairielike expanse, to the head of the glacier, and then we soar alongside the spectacular spire of Mount Cook, New Zealand's tent-shaped crown. In a matter of seconds, a pattern forms out of the chaos, like a picture slipping into place in a kaleidoscope, and the flow from snowy peak to glacier to sea makes sense. As the winds that whip around the mountain buffet us, I finger my seat belt nervously.

chapter eight

I NEED ALL THE ALP I CAN GET

The explorers of the past were great men, and we should honor them. But let us not forget that their spirit lives on.

—Sir Edmund Hillary

He toki kei runga, he toki kei raro.

An ax above, an ax below.

Too often the past seems like a foreign country to me, but this flight elicits an avalanche of memory shards. I had been to this mountain many years before on a different quest.

From what little I know of the concept, I would venture that if there is one non-Māori who embodies the spirit of kaitiakitanga in an ecumenical and universally recognized way, it is Ed Hillary. In 1953, during the same week Queen Elizabeth II was crowned, the lanky thirty-three-year-old New Zealand beekeeper reached the angular summit of Mount Everest, the world's highest peak, and became an icon of global consciousness. Unlike most who achieve wide fame and fortune at a young age, Ed did not fritter away his renown on vanity or self-gratification. He decided to give back to the mountain that gave him repute and to the people who guided him to the top: the Sherpas of the Khumbu region of Nepal. So he spent the next forty years building schools, roads, and clinics throughout the Himalayas, and has made more of a difference than any single human being in the improvement and well-being of this high land and its inhabitants.

But while many who revere what Ed has accomplished follow in his crowning footsteps on Everest, I decided to travel to Mount Cook (12,316 feet) on the South Island of New Zealand, where Ed cut his eyeteeth as a climber. My goal was to shamble solo up the South Ridge of the Cook massif, the route he pioneered back when he was an unknown outdoor enthusiast. My plan was to follow in the Big Man's boot steps at a different time from the madding crowd—in June, which is midwinter in New Zealand—to ensure solitude.

Long before Ed became famous, he was a young Auckland air navigator who would use his spare time to slip away and make solo expeditions, often in June, because he found winter climbing greatly to his taste.

Mount Cook (12,316 feet) on the South Island of New Zealand, where Ed Hillary cut his eyeteeth as a climber

When I made that first sortie to Mount Cook, I arrived at The Hermitage Hotel, a half mile high at the base of the big hill—the same hotel that was Ed's base in February 1948, when he made his assault on the South Ridge. It is now in Aoraki–Mount Cook National Park, 174,694 acres at the end of a found poem of a road that follows the shore of Lake Pukaki. New Zealand established the park in 1953, the same year Ed topped Everest.

Outside, the sun was estival, yet the snow-laden landscape looked brutally brumal, like a Northern European Christmas setting. I could see the icy wedge of Mount Cook from my frosted window, including the dead-white summit itself, that generous scoop of vanilla ice cream where all the ridgelines meet.

There are New Zealanders who have been to Mount Cook a score of times and have never seen the white roof of their country, so I felt lucky for the large slice of good weather and was eager to get outside. After a shower and a meat pie, I wandered over to Alpine Guides and went over my plans with Bryan Carter, who was not keen on the concept of a solo hike up the Hooker Glacier, the route Ed used to make his ascent. The trail was unmarked in the deep snow, and this was the height of avalanche season. "You can make it to the lake, but don't go any farther. Definitely don't try to make the Hooker Hut," he warned. With these words, I retreated to the local stop for thirsty adventurers: The Tavern Bar in The Hermitage, where I spent the afternoon and evening exploring the contour lines of peanut bowls and frosted glasses of Speight's beer.

The morning next, my breakfast was a breath of fresh air and a good look around. I pulled on a pair of long Capilene underwear, struggled into my GORE-TEX expedition suit, and wrapped it all in a hefty down jacket before stepping from the reasonable into the extreme. The air beyond the hotel door was so cold it fizzled and snapped; every breath seemed to cut my throat. Fresh snow coated the landscape. Just off the hotel terrace, a sign marked the way to the Hooker Valley Track, and I followed its direction across the tufted flats toward the low moraines east of White Horse Hill. In a short time, I passed the site of the original Hermitage, a simple cob-wall cottage built in 1884.

For the next thirty minutes, though I was surrounded by power-ful peaks, I could not see the pyramidal mountain I had come to climb. On my left, I passed the stone Alpine Memorial, dedicated to Londoner

Sydney King and local guides Darby Thomson and Jock Richmond, who were swept away by an avalanche in 1914 and became the first of many climbers to die on Mount Cook.

I didn't stop, instead picking up the pace as I passed through broken, hummocky hills walled by the low lines of morainic boulders. These moraines were the marks of different phases of glacier advance and retreat, which even in recent times have greatly altered the landscape. Gone was the arch spread across the snout of the Mueller Glacier beneath hundred-foot ice cliffs. The arch had greeted gold-seeker Julius von Haast when he wandered into this vault of nature in 1862. He was so impressed with the valley and its main glacier that he named them after the distinguished botanist of the day Sir William J. Hooker.

Gone, too, was the ice bridge over the Hooker River, which before 1900 enabled merino sheep from Birch Hill Run to be put to summer pasture on the upper Hooker flats. And Te Waewae Glacier above Stocking Stream no longer looked like a stocking; ice retreat had unraveled its foot and lower leg.

I came to a bridge of four cables stretched some forty feet across and fifteen feet above the daunting drainage of the Cook massif. The bottom two cables supported a wire-mesh walkway, while the upper pair served as handrails. I wobbled and bounced across, keeping a wary eye on the rushing glacial waters, which threw blasts of refrigerated air my way. Once across, I turned back and looked down the valley across to the hotel's backdrop—the Sealy Range. There, amid the serrated skyline, was the undistinguished Mount Olivier, the first real mountain Ed Hillary climbed as a lad on a short vacation in 1939. The impetuous and kinetic Hillary dashed to its summit, leaving in the dust the mountain guide he had hired. "It was the happiest day I had ever spent," he later said.

Just before the second swing bridge, I passed a shingle cliff festooned with icicles and snapped one off to suck on as I walked. Halfway across the bridge, I stopped and grabbed the railings tightly. An ominous crack resounded and rolled into a deep rumble. I looked around in time to see a puff and then a slow cascade of white: an avalanche crashing down the eastern wall of Mount Sefton. At 10,355 feet, it was a little smaller than Mount Cook, but just as louche and dangerous. From here, it was just half a head turn away.

Once across the bridge, I tramped up the valley and turned a corner. Presently, the perfect pyramid of Mount Cook, permanently coiffed in snow and ice, burst into view—just as it had to Ed Hillary more than half a century ago, and to Māori well before him. Māori called it Aorangi, or "cloud piercer." In 1851 it was officially named Mount Cook after the great Yorkshire navigator, who never saw his namesake. It was christened by Captain J. L. Stokes of the HMS *Acheron,* who spied the peak while sailing down the west coast. In 1998, it was officially rechristened Aoraki–Mount Cook to include a version of the Māori name. At 12,316 feet (formerly 12,349 feet), Mount Cook is the tallest mountain in New Zealand, and taller than any Australian mountain for that matter. But Cook is only one of nineteen ice-draped peaks taller than ten thousand feet in the Southern Alps, the sharp spine of mountain country that runs the length of the South Island. This range amply illustrates the effects of the Pacific tectonic plate grinding against the Indian-Australian plate. Every year, New Zealand experiences some sixteen thousand earthquakes, and the Southern Alps are pushed about four inches higher.

In this insubordinate land, ever clacking at the sky, the contours rise so quickly that the two-mile-high peaks are within twenty miles of the sea. The steep terrains, combined with the heavy rains of the Roaring Forties, as the southern latitudes are called, have created hundreds of glaciers. Nowhere else on earth are so many glaciers at so low an altitude, and it is here that global warming has a face. And I was heading for a pock on that face: the Hooker Glacier.

The Hooker, like the other glaciers here, was created by the vast precipitation—as much as three hundred inches a year—that falls on its névé and slowly compresses to form blue-tinted, oxygen-rich ice that flows downhill under its own weight.

Māori have a more lyrical explanation. To them, this river of ice is Ka Roimata o Hinehukatere, or "the tears of the avalanche girl." Hinehukatere and her lover, Tawe, who hated the mountains, were climbing high one day when he slipped and was lost. She cries to this day, and her tears freeze to form the glacier.

Hillary probably didn't care too much about myths when he approached this sea of ruptured ice. His mind was focused on higher ground. Mountains were there to be climbed, and climb them he would, without the frills.

Despite the continuous mountain-building that takes place here at the margins of the Pacific and Indian–Australian plates, the brooding peak rising from this valley was not any higher than when Ed was here; in fact, it was appreciably smaller. A little after midnight on December 14, 1991, the top of Mount Cook collapsed like an overcooked cake, creating an enormous rock avalanche down the East Face. About fifteen million cubic yards of rock and snow plummeted down a fifty-seven-degree slope, traveling at two hundred to three hundred miles per hour for more than four miles and missing several climbing parties asleep in the Plateau Hut by less than a thousand feet. Māori claimed the mountain crumbled because those who employed its slopes, virtually all white men, did not pay proper respect nor make any efforts to steward the peak nor do anything to improve it. As a result, the great mountain was thirty-three feet shorter. It was getting closer in height to Mount Tasman, New Zealand's second-highest peak at 11,475 feet.

Which brings to mind another polemic. Suppose Mount Everest turned out not to be the highest spot on the planet, and Pakistan's K2 proved higher? For years, scientists have debated the respective heights, now officially 29,022.6 feet for Everest and 28,268 feet for K2. On a 1986 expedition, after measuring electromagnetic signals from a satellite, Seattle astronomer George Wallerstein calculated that K2 had an elevation of 29,064 feet, a few steps above Everest's dénouement. If Everest is indeed the king, as the latest laser survey suggests, what if an avalanche brought down the top few hundred feet, and K2 emerged supreme?

The author in the footsteps of the Big Man,
Ed Hillary, up the Hooker Glacier on Mount Cook

Where would that leave Edmund Hillary in the history books? What would become of the whole romantic narrative of mountaineering? Can anyone—outside of alpine enthusiasts—name the men who first climbed K2, which is considered the

63

tougher challenge, regardless of height? (They were Italians Achille Compagnoni and Lino Lacedelli, who reached the steep summit of gleaming ice that straddles the Sino-Pakistani border on July 31, 1954.)

In the week before Christmas in 1988, I was in New Delhi sharing dinner with Ed and the woman who would soon become his wife, June. He was the New Zealand ambassador to India, Nepal, and Bangladesh, a seemingly unlikely job for a mountain climber. But no Westerner was more revered in these parts, and when he spoke, half a world listened. I gave him a book I had written a few years before about rivers down which I had made the exploratory descents, geographic firsts in some ways perhaps like his own. (A tough river never before navigated was often called "the Mount Everest of rivers" by river clan insiders.)

Rivers, though, have never offered the linear purity of mountains, and because they are ever moving, there's no there there. Not surprisingly, no waterway has ever captured the world's imagination in the same way Everest has. Seventeen well-equipped expeditions straddling fifty years tried to climb Everest before Hillary, and all failed, with many deaths. No river exploration has created such a catalog. Beyond that, I could never pretend to equate my own wanderings with Ed's crowning feat, nor with the great works he undertook thereafter.

Yet, just when I wanted to ask him how he ended up on top of the world, he paused, turning his attention from his lamb curry, and catechized in his thistle-dry accent, "Why you? Why were you, of all the river runners around, the first to negotiate these rivers?"

"It was just luck," I answered. "It could have been anyone. I was at the right place at the right time."

Ed understood. His caterpillar-like salt-and-pepper eyebrows shot hairs in all directions. The bags under his flickering eyes were nearly as eloquent as the eyes themselves.

He knew about luck. He knew how easily someone else's name could have entered the pantheon of knighted heroes. He knew that the good weather was a roll of the dice that went his way, and that even from a publicity standpoint, his timing could not have been more fortuitous: the news of his success reached England the night before the coronation of Elizabeth II, a convergence of triumph for a fading empire. Ed never claimed to be the world's greatest climber; he was just the first white man on the highest real estate on earth.

And yet, unlike many who have had greatness thrust upon them, he didn't see his life go downhill after his peak experience. He returned

The Southern Alps, the sharp spine of mountain country that runs the length of the South Island. This range amply illustrates the effects of the Pacific tectonic plate grinding against the Indian–Australian plate.

65

to the Himalayas again and again, in a less-glamorous fashion, to help the Sherpas build schools, hospitals, bridges, and freshwater pipelines and to participate in reforestation projects, in the true spirit of kaitiakitanga, leaving the land better than he found it.

And as if to acknowledge this extra-mundane and supernal effort, this pay-it-forward exercise, the land gave back with interest to Ed when he needed it. Ten years after his historic summit, Ed came back to Everest to climb when suddenly he suffered high-altitude sickness, the deadly mountain edema that can kill in short order. He was taken down to a nearby clinic and was revived. When he was well again, he discovered that the clinic that saved his life was one that he had built for the local Khumbu Sherpas.

I continued my hike through flats and terraces in an area I knew was splashed in early summer with the colors of the Mount Cook lily (the largest ranunculus in the world) and other wildflowers. Now, in June, there were only spectral whites and mournful grays. I followed the tracks of an unknown cross-country skier who had followed the Hooker River, milky from the rock flour ground by the glacier. Ed himself had skied the Hooker on about this same date back in 1949. As I got closer, I could hear the glacier talking to itself in loud cracks and gurgles. I looked up. With the dramatically symmetrical Mount Cook in my gaze and dozens of shimmering, high mountains enveloping me, I felt as if I were in some sublime, alien world.

My sense of scale was lost. This was just too immense, too awesome for the brain to properly process. Mount Cook's spectacularly creased peak looked as if it were a stone's throw away. The Hooker Glacier stretched in front of me, part of it studded with ice pillars, some of it smooth and sparkling in the sun, and some swept into stiff peaks and ridges, looking as if someone had taken a pogo stick through a field of meringue. I could see the wind spinning snow off Mount Sefton. At first I thought it was another avalanche, but it made no sound, and the snow plume didn't let up. I realized then that the effect was created by a high and powerful wind, one the villagers call a nor'wester.

I proceeded through the ever-deepening snow until I reached the terminal lake. This was the point at which I was supposed to turn back. The skinny ski tracks did an abrupt 180-degree turn here. A park-service sign warned: "AVALANCHE ZONE! HAZARDOUS ROUTE AHEAD. TRACK CLOSED BEYOND HOOKER TERMINAL LAKE DUE TO AVALANCHE DANGER."

Ed had encountered similar warning signs back in 1948, though they were unwritten. But he didn't turn back. Not here, not on Everest. I, too, ploughed on.

Because the lake was frozen, I figured its surface would be the easiest route across. I stepped onto it. Treading lightly along the glaze, I made good progress. About halfway across its length, I heard a sound like shattering glass. I looked down and saw a web of cracks appear around my boots. Gingerly, I took another step. The ice began to indent as more wrinkles appeared on the surface. The water beneath the ice emitted a dull, digestive growl. This would not do. Alone and in midwinter, I could not afford to fall into a glacial lake. I inched back and over to the lateral moraine shore and scrambled up a scree slope, slipping back a foot for every three upward. Consisting chiefly of sedimentary rock called greywacke—hard sandstone and siltstone about 200 million years old—Mount Cook was not built to last. Kiwis call this stuff I was trying to scale "Weet-Bix," after a popular breakfast cereal with about the same texture, strength, and, Kellogg's might say, taste.

I paused at a long, crooked crease in the snow. Perhaps it was the trail. It was impossible to tell with certainty because the snow was several feet deep. But every fifty yards or so a marker, either a stone cairn or a five-foot metal bar, stuck out jaggedly like a broken bone through skin. Using these markers as guides, I slowly hoisted myself up into the impressive but forbidding wasteland.

Soon I was beyond the lake in the ablation zone, adjacent to the Hooker. I stepped onto the pleats of the mountain's skirt. The glacier looked to be less than a hundred feet thick where its liquid runoff melted into the gray lake, but upstream I knew it was almost a thousand feet thick and a quarter mile wide in places. The Empress, Noeline, and Mona glaciers, pushing down from Endeavour Col (named for Captain Cook's converted coal ship) on the Mount Cook Range, all swung southward, combining into one great ice fall: the short, steep, and thick Hooker Glacier.

At the head of the Hooker, Ed first proved his mountain mettle—and his possession of the vital spark of kaitiakitanga. Just three days after his successful climb of the South Ridge, he was off again, this time with friends, up beyond the glacier's head. When one of his climbing partners, Ruth Adams, slipped and fell sixty feet, Ed stayed with her while others went for help. With terrific energy, he hacked out an ice cave six by four by four feet, breaking his ice ax in the process. He nursed the badly injured woman for twelve hours, until ten that night, when a rescuer showed up with a sleeping bag. It took another week to get her off the mountain. Ruth Adams went on to become a respected doctor who saved many lives, and an environmentalist who worked to protect the wilds of the South Island. The land and its inhabitants are better for her touch.

68

I continued to wade through the snow, each leg movement a ritualistic gesture, like a benediction without a recipient. Then a cotton-wool silence overtook me at once. It was so total my ears roared—or was that another avalanche? I saw blood. The footprints of a European hare ran parallel to my own for a good thirty yards, then ended at a sprawled mark in the snow soaked with red stains. A harrier hawk? The haunting, raven-like, native morepork? The New Zealand falcon? Perhaps it was the kea, the cheeky alpine parrot that was forever picking apart the rubber on vehicle windshield wipers in the park. The distinction mattered little to the vanished victim.

I knew the Hooker Hut was not far away. I looked at my watch: 2 p.m. I had been hiking steadily for four hours, so if I turned back then I would arrive at The Hermitage just at dark. However, I knew this was to be a full-moon night, and I hoped to make the hut as a private goal, my own summit. Then again, the clear weather was reportedly due to end, and storms often scampered in swiftly and violently.

Suddenly I seemed to have slipped into Antarctica. The temperature dropped to deep freeze. I was in the wind zone I had seen miles down the valley. Huge hurricanes of snow were swooping down the slopes, crashing about my ears and slapping across my cheekbones. Ice clung to my face like a strange, blistering growth. Vision was impaired, but as I squinted I could see Mount Cook ahead, looking very much like the Paramount Pictures logo. But now clouds poured over the pinnacle ridge, and Mount Cook seemed to sway and begin to topple, closing the gap of stark sky over my head. Beneath the howls of the icy wind I could hear the deep rumbles of the Hooker Glacier. These were perfect windslab avalanche conditions. The fresh, dry, blown snow had built up on a hard base on the abrupt slopes above me, and a layer could release at any time. Still, I felt lucky, and persisted.

The snow was now often waist deep, and it took an effort just to move a few yards. Nonetheless, in the spirit of Hillary I carried on, stiff (and frozen) upper lip, using the metal rod markers as short-term goals. But then I fell into a snowdrift and emerged to scan the landscape through the blinding snow. I searched and searched, but in the cold, marble light could find no signs of a marker, no indication of a route upward. I backtracked a few yards and was still lost, and when I scrambled to the top of a boulder, where I was barely able to hold on in the gale-force winds, I remained in the dark. What would Ed have done? Continued, no doubt, with little thought. It was like beekeeping: if you dwell on the concept it becomes too frightening. You just do it.

The elusive hut in summertime is really not much of a challenge to reach, requiring just a walk to the head of the valley, where the climbing then gets serious. It was still not in sight. No doubt it was just around the alpine spur, an ace and a few minutes away. But I couldn't go on. I was, after all, a mountaineer manqué. Edmund Hillary was something altogether different, part of a historical narrative that is essentially over. He was a figure in the story of heroic adventure that included Marco Polo, Columbus, Lewis and Clark, Stanley and Livingstone, Peary and Scott, Amundsen, Lindbergh—men with knives in their teeth and ice in their beards and in their veins. When Ed climbed here, he belonged to a time when "because it is there" was a good enough reason to climb a mountain. People are more "enlightened" now. To many, such adventurism seems boyishly foolish, environmentally unsound. It is no longer man against nature; rather, it must be with nature, or nothing at all.

I turned back.

Four hours later, après-glacier, I was in The Hermitage Hotel's luxurious Tavern Bar in front of a blazing fire sipping mulled wine. I gave the barkeep a New Zealand $5 note, which featured the face of the country's most famous mountaineer on its front, a currency for all time. The place was, after all, better for Ed having been here, and many other places were, too.

The soul of the Southern Alps

IMMACULATE CONFECTION

Ngā kōtuku awe nui o te uru
Ka moe whakaaio ki te mate.

The long-plumed white herons of the west
Sleep peacefully in death.

From Franz Josef, we continue north along a luxurious folded coast where the plants have forgotten their manners and behave like trees. At one curve we pass the small settlement of Okarito, a former gold-mining township that its peak housed one thousand five hundred people. Now only about thirty folks remain, including Booker Prize winner Keri Hulme. This is also the edge of the Okarito Lagoon, the largest unmodified wetland in New Zealand, covering three thousand hectares of shallow open water and tidal flats. While it is estimated that by 1770 about half of New Zealand's bird species were dispatched forever by human meddling, one wouldn't get that impression here. More than seventy bird species have been identified in the area, from black swans to bitterns, tui, bellbirds, pigeons, robins, and keas—and, Ian tells me, this is the home of the kotuku, the rare and much-revered white heron. Māori believe this bird carries their deceased spirits northward to the spirit tree, where the spirits rest before making the final voyage back to the homeland. Ian says Māori believe they will see the heron just once in a lifetime, often just before the big journey. We see none as we curve through the wetlands.

Farther up the road, we pass through the little village of Ross, which for a time equaled its Marin County, California, counterpart in wealth, as it sits on New Zealand's richest alluvial gold field. Here, in 1907, a ninety-nine-ounce nugget was found, the country's largest ever. It ended up as a coronation gift to King George V, who melted it to make royal tableware at Buckingham Palace.

Late in the day we cross the Arahura River and look down into water that seems to glow with fluorescence.

History, it is said, is written by the victors. History, it is also assumed, is written by cultures with a written language. Māori defied these conventions with a language of stone. For millennia, Māori passed on stories, myths, and tropes through their intricate carvings in beautiful greenstone, which was mined in abundance in this river.

Kaitiakitanga, Ian tells me, is not just about the land. It is also about preserving customs and a unique and elaborate culture. Pounamu, or greenstone, holds great meaning for Māori, and it was in many ways responsible for lifting the development of the people in the way that steel did for Europeans. Not only was it used for tools, weapons, and art, but also the carvings were a way to continue an exuberant civilization.

According to legend, Poutini was a giant water being and the protector of greenstone. He abducted a beautiful woman from the North Island and fled south, pursued by her husband. Poutini hid with his captive in the bed of the Arahura River. To avoid capture, Poutini transformed the woman into his own spiritual essence—greenstone—and fled downriver to the sea. The woman became the mother lode of all greenstone, and Poutini continues to swim up and down the west coast protecting the spirit of this stone.

"I know a kaitiaki for the pounamu here," Ian tells me with a conspiratorial lean. "I'll take you to him."

Just beyond the Arahura, we turn into the Awatuna Homestead, a two-story timber lodge owned by Hēmi and Pauline Te Rākau. Hēmi, Ian informs me, is a kaitiaki of much *mana,* which is, I believe, a sort of clout or power that comes from beyond this world. During the intertribal wars of earlier centuries, Māori would eat the brains of the conquered to get their mana.

It is dark when we trundle in through an old gateway, and Hēmi dashes out to greet us. "Kia ora," he says, his orotund voice swelling. He rigorously shakes my hand while welcoming me in Te Reo Māori, then cants forward and presses his prowlike nose against mine three times in a traditional greeting gesture known as a *hongi*. It is the mingling of breath between the two people, representing unity. The first press is a greeting to the person, the second acknowledges ancestors, and the third, involving the nose and forehead, honors life in this world. He also insists I put my hand on his shoulder during the ritual, a gesture meant to prove I don't have a weapon behind my back. He then steps back and translates, "I welcome you from the depth of my heart to these gardens and this home. Nothing will harm you here tonight. You will sleep safely and like a baby."

It turns out that though Hēmi has lived in Awatuna for most of his adult life, he hails from the Ngāti Pakau *hapū* (subtribe), affiliated with the Ngā Puhi (primary tribe) in the far north of New Zealand. For most of his career, he was a cultural adviser to the Department of Conservation, where he often clashed with official policy and fought for the Māori perspective to be represented in government corridors and edicts. He also stood on the edge of the canyon that separates conservation from kaitiakitanga.

As we pause at the portico of his living room, Hēmi clarifies the chasm:

"The concepts start off with a commonality, and they have an end goal which appears to be similar, but kaitiakitanga is based on tradition, on a belief system of a whole people. It has its own rules and regulations. It has people within that system who are responsible for certain things to be in place at all times, no matter what adversity may appear. The essence of kaitiakitanga is to look at the resource—a fishery, a forest, even the inanimate ones: stones or mountains or those from the other world—and shift thinking with whatever the perceived threat happens to be: climate, land use, economics, politics, the ever-changing circumstances of life.

"Conservation, on the other hand, has an element of absolutism. There can be quite a dogged, fixed goal, regardless of other factors, and that goal must be achieved, perhaps to the detriment of other things. So while they appear to have a commonality, in my view they are two distinct systems in the way solutions are enacted. Kaitiakitanga molds with the problem of the day. The rules and regulations within kaitiakitanga don't change, but the circumstances may. Kaitiakitanga is more woven into the thought or feelings of the people. It can get very heated, of course, especially when it comes to issues of traditional ownership of land and alienation from the past. Conservation is a wonderful concept, but it is really driven by passion, wanting to save something at all costs. It's often forbidding in the 'you can never use this' sense. Kaitiakitanga is more balanced. It's an expectation of wise use, and it's one of the support beams that hold up our culture."

Modern conservation, some argue, is really a manifestation of the Christian design of redemption, trying to make good for all the bad previously inflicted. Māori theology, however, doesn't take the sunset personally; rather, it sees all as part of a natural ebb and flow that if respected ends in a net balance.

European versus Māori weapons. The Māori used a mere pounamu. It looks like decorative art, but in fact it is a deadly weapon.

Hēmi's views did not always sit well with the Department of Conservation. So he took early retirement in 2004 and decided to open his home to guests so he could demonstrate Māori hospitality and put some of his belief systems into practice. When not hosting and interpreting, he pursues his other passion, a modern version of crafting wood or stone: rebuilding Morris Eight tourers. He is a kaitiaki of small prewar vintage cars.

Inside his cozy ménage, in front of a blazing fire, over a glass of New World Pinot Noir, I ask Hēmi what it means to be a kaitiaki. He looks as though he had stepped off the curb to hail a cab and had been hit by a bus. No visiting Pakeha has ever broached this question.

He cocks his head in thought and then gives forth a magisterial, erudite tour of an unfamiliar world. He says there is a spiritual dimension—that it is a bit like being a museum curator, but that while a curator takes care of physical things and has no personal relationship with his charges, this goes much, much deeper. "A kaitiaki is an agent in a caring system for anything important for the greater good; it is an obligation to assure continuance of the principles and practices that will allow food, sleep, and shelter for all people and all time. It is a caretaker and an instrument of balance, a holistic planner."

But a kaitiaki is not just a human agent, he explicates. It can be a rock in a harbor that guides boats in. It can be a tree that shades a garden. Or it can be a stone—and he picks up a piece of volcanic glass the size of bread loaf, sliced in half by a diamond saw. It is greenstone, worn by the nearby Arahura River. "This piece belongs to one of my children. The other half to another child who is far away. But they can each touch the stone and touch the sibling. But when we gather in one place, we put the stones together, and it makes the family strong."

Then he picks up off his table a rounded, carved stone that looks like a fraternity hazing paddle. He turns it in his hand. It is about twenty inches long and three-fourths of an inch thick in the middle, the blade about four inches wide, tapering on either side to a tolerably sharp edge. Hēmi says it is called a *mere pounamu* and is a "cultural hinge," connecting his kin through time. It looks like decorative art, but in fact it is a deadly weapon, a combination cudgel and ax used in hand-to-hand warfare. A warrior would stun an opponent with a blow to the temple, then cut through his neck with the leading edge.

Hēmi slowly draws his hand down the side of the spatulate stone, explaining that it took a long time to carve each mere—often months or years, even generations, carving in the evenings, as there were no televisions or computers. Pounamu contains toxic, asbestos-like fibers, so the stone had to be carved underwater, using sandstone as emery. Mere like this, like all greenstone, became valuable trade items, often chiefly as tokens. They gave the owners mana and acted as protectors, as kaitiaki. "This greenstone has its own life," Hēmi asserts.

The declaration fills a silent room like water pouring into a bowl. After a few beats, I pull from under my sweater the stylized greenstone fishhook that Kylie had given me at Lake Wanaka. Hēmi examines it and smiles with eyes as clear as creek water. "It denotes chiefdomship. It is a sacred replica of the hook that our ancient relative, Maui, used when he stood here on the South Island and fished the North Island up from the sea. And it too is a kaitiaki, a guardian of fish, a supplier of food. So don't wear it if you go swimming in the sea, as it belongs to the sea, and the sea might take it, and you, back."

And then Hēmi falls back into Māori: "Kia whakatu tika te taiao me te taiao tiaki te taiao," which he translates as: "If the environment is kept well and strong, it will look after itself."

And for a moment I can't tell if the maxims are coming from Oprah or Daryl Hannah or a bumper sticker or an ancient ethnic bloodline; but no matter the origins, they all look backward and forward to balance.

The heart of Mount Aspiring National Park

TALL TAILS

Kia mau mai ki ngā tātai whetu e tatu atu ki ngā mea katoa.

Hold fast to the genealogy lines from the stars to oneself
and all things.

n the morning, from my room I can faintly make out Hēmi's muffled voice the way an underwater swimmer hears sounds from above the surface. He seems in a quiet conversation, perhaps with his wife, or a stone. I can make out one word: "Kaitiakitanga."

The early day imparts a blushed calm, in contrast to Ian's shirt, which represents a personal threat to the ozone layer. We belt back some coffee, give our heartfelt thanks to Hēmi and Pauline, and head to the vehicle to voyage north. Ian captains our car as if it were a sailing ship in a squall, skirring by paddocks of Romney sheep, bright pastures of Holstein-Friesian cattle, and waves of unpremeditated woodlands. We slip into an agrestic mood. Then, at the town of Hokitika, we board a transcountry puddle hopper (New Zealand is never more than two hundred miles wide) and fly over the shimmering Southern Alps to the east coast garden conurbation of Christchurch, second-largest city in the country. It was an early environmental consciousness, quite against the grain, that gave this place its enduring garden character. In 1870, ornithologist Thomas Potts championed the establishing of botanical plots here, writing with coauthor W. Gray: "The constantly recurring bush fires, the means by which the tenant of crown lands seeks to improve the condition and quality of the grasses for the depasturing of his stock, and the wasteful management of the once magnificently timbered forests threaten at no distant period the almost entire destruction of many interesting and valuable species."

We rent a car and sally north some more, to a place called Te Ahi-kai-koura-a-Tama-ki-te-rangi, which means "the fire that cooked the crayfish of Tama ki te Rangi."

The story goes that Tama ki te Rangi was an ancient Māori chief who couldn't control his women. While pursuing his runaway wives, he stopped here to eat some crayfish. He got his retribution, though, when the wives were transformed into greenstone on the other side of the island.

Thankfully, the town today is more commonly known as "Kaikoura" and has a reputation for having adopted the values of kaitiakitanga as a community ethic. If recycling is part of this ethic, then it must be true, as I notice that all the public trash-disposal sites have five different containers: one each for cans, waste, food, plastic, and glass. The township of Kaikoura sits on a siltstone peninsula that juts out from the snow-collared Seaward Kaikoura Ranges, a spur of the Southern Alps, and according to legend was carved out by a Māori god with a magic sword.

At the verge of a forest called the Puhipuhi Scenic Reserve, we meet Ian's old friend Maurice Manawatu, a descendant of Paikea, "The Whale Rider." It is a triumph of legend over history that this story is so globally regarded—the tale of a young Pacific Islander called Paikea who was rescued by the whale Tohora and carried on its back to the settlement of Whangara on the North Island.

Paikea was the youngest and favorite son of the chief Uenuku from the island of MaNgāia in the present-day Cook Islands. This favoritism made Paikea's elder brothers excessively jealous. They conspired to kill Paikea while fishing offshore and tell Uenuku he drowned.

Driving past bright fields and pastures, past rolls of hay bundled like gumdrops

But the night before the trip, Paikea feigned sleep and overheard his brothers plotting. Far out to sea, Paikea foiled their plan by deliberately sinking the canoe and drowning his brothers.

Adrift in the mixing ocean, Paikea clung to a canoe plank and awaited his own death. Then Tohora the whale appeared, lifted Paikea onto his great back, and carried him to the promising land of New Zealand.

Years later, one of Paikea's sons, Tahupōtiki, traveled farther south to Kaikoura and became a founder of the South Island tribe Ngāi Tahu.

Maurice started a company called Māori Tours Kaikorua, which conducts small-group tours that share local Māori history and interpret Māori consanguinity with the environment today. Maurice says that his lineage has been traced back twenty-two generations, but that thirty years ago his culture was almost rubbed out. He has started this company to help with the revival. He offers to take us for a walk in the woods, and we step into a dark and thaumaturgic place. A short way into the trees, Maurice turns to me and begins a long monologue in Te Reo Māori, beetling along, sometimes hissing through his missing teeth. He seems to go for minutes. As he rolls on, I look at the sky, at my boots, at his boots. Finally he winds down and takes a breath, as though tasting the air, and I take the moment to ask for an interpretation.

He replies: "I said, 'Welcome!'"

After further probing, he explains that the greeting acknowledges his *whakapapa,* his oral genealogy, which includes his *maunga* (a sacred mountain that overlooks Kaikoura), then his *awa* (the river that spills down its flanks), his waka (the canoe that brought his ancestors here), and his *iwi* (tribe). Whakapapa binds all people to a common source. He asks me then to make my introduction. I do so: "My sacred mountain is Rainier; my river is Columbia; my ancestors' canoe was the *Mayflower*; and my tribe is Bangs."

The tour has a scripted quality, but still it is compelling and allows a glimpse into a culture so different from my own. Maurice decides to bestow on me a Māori name: "Ono." Not because of any biblical connotations, I am grateful to learn, but because it is Māori for "six," a number of good fortune that seems to cross cultural lines.

Maurice's business is a familial imperative, and as we stroll through this version of Shakespeare's magical forest, his well-tattooed first cousin, Kim Kahu, tells me about various trees and plants. The *kawa kawa* plant, also known as the New Zealand pepper tree, has twenty-seven medicinal uses, including suppressing coughs and colds and, if rendered into tea, purifying blood. You can bathe in a solution made from the leaves to alleviate skin problems such as eczema, she says. She also points out how holey many of the leaves are. They do have a seraphic glow, but she means that they have been gnawed by bugs. She advises that these are the healthiest leaves, because the bugs know their stuff, and so if one is preparing a bath or tea, these are the ones to use. Of course, because early Māori had no written language, the trials and errors of ethnobotany were passed down orally through the *tohunga,* or medicine man, and mistakes were no doubt made with some of the poisonous native plants. One beautiful plant called *poroporo,* a type of nightshade, has purplish stems, trumpet-shaped, mauve flowers with yellow centers, and tasty-looking but deadly oval green berries.

Maurice pulls out a flask, says he has prepared a tea from some of these native plants, and pours some into a plastic glass. It tastes crisp, like lime juice.

"What you may find, in about five minutes once the tea kicks in," Maurice says, lowering his face after I have downed the brew like a kea swooping in on its prey, "is that you might start to hear voices in your head and see rainbows in the trees, and when that happens just go with it."

I flash back a look that I imagine telegraphs both concern and anticipation, and he responds, "Nah; I wouldn't do that." Maurice, it seems, is able to juggle a scientific sensibility with a pastiche of Māori myths the

way chefs at Benihana toss big knives—with precision and a show-man's wink that makes his little tour fun.

Next, we stop to fondle a fern Maurice says is feared throughout the sport-ing world, the ponga, or silver fern (*Cyathea dealbata*), which is the emblem on the jerseys of the All Blacks, the New Zealand national rugby union team (the

Maurice Manawatu, a descendant of Paikea, "The Whale Rider." "The whales were once kaitiaki *for us," Maurice says. "But then they were hunted for a long time, and Māori were as involved as anyone. They were almost hunted away. But now we are the* kaitiaki *for whales, and they are coming back."*

national basketball team is called the Tall Blacks). Ian pipes up: "Rugby is not a matter of life and death here. It's more important than that."

Māori legend has it that the silver fern once lived in the sea but made the move to the forest when a lost Māori asked it to come and be a guide. Thereafter, hunters and warriors would bend the fronds and turn the silver side up so the moonlight would illuminate the way home.

This is the same fern whose leaf I had tossed over my shoulder while rafting the Kaituna River, its wrong-side-up landing foreboding bad luck which, thankfully, didn't happen. It's a riot of a plant that can grow up to thirty feet in height, and its silver-white coloration makes it useful for marking trails during night walking.

We continue the hike deeper into the woods. It is like walking through the entrails of a giant beast, a dim, tangled labyrinth of vines and giant trees that block out the sun, a place where gnomes and goblins crouch and creep. Inexplicable sounds come from the depths: crashes, cawing, screeching, sudden rushes in the undergrowth, and rustling high in the canopy.

As I feel for the ground with each footfall, I sense I am part of a ceremony I don't understand. Where to put my feet? What to touch or not? Is something hidden ahead?

At last we stop in front of an enormous, dark tree, and I inhale its earthly vesper fragrance. Maurice considers the wood and then tells me it is roughly five hundred years old. It is a matai, or black pine. Though once in abundance, matai-dominated forests are now a rarity. Like other New Zealand podocarps, matai has very fine timber qualities. The wood is durable with a satiny finish, a top choice for flooring and weatherboards. In the early 1900s, most native forests were logged, by both Pakeha and

Māori, but when a school was built for the children of the lumberjacks, a playground grove was kept intact and protected—and we are standing in that playground. A little farther down the path is what Maurice calls "the Big Chief," a reddish-gray tōtara tower with no hint of taper and bark that is thick, corky, furrowed, and stringy. The wood is ideal for roof shingles and carving and was a favorite of early Māori. It looks very much like a tree I've seen in Chile, *Podocarpus nubigenus,* which of course bolsters the argument that South America and New Zealand were part of the super-continent Gondwanaland some one hundred million years in the past. To call a Māori a tōtara is the highest compliment in these parts, and when an elder of stature dies, the salute is: "Another tōtara has fallen."

Māori oral tradition tells that as saplings, tōtara were marked by the forefathers so that when, centuries later, they were used to make canoes, the marking-induced weakness in the grain would make the work of carving easier. This was a commitment to time horizons of up to twelve generations, a pay-it-forward concept ingrained in the culture.

Just then, as if on cue, a little, multicolored bird chirps and flits around in short, acrobatic circles, then opens its tail proudly. Maurice says it is a tiwakawaka, a pied fantail of the flycatcher family. Maurice says to watch the frantic movements of the bird because they are replicated in the famous *haka* warrior dances.

Tiwakawaka, it turns out, is also the name of a grandson of the demigod Maui, who, the story goes, placed his foot on the Kai-koura peninsula to steady himself while he hauled up the fish that became the North Island. The grandson was one of the first settlers to arrive in New Zealand some one thousand years ago (give or take, depending on which anthropology/history/mythology you subscribe to), well before main migrations. When a canoe carrying another Polynesian explorer landed, Tiwakawaka came down to the beach to challenge the seafarer, jumping side to side and slashing his stick through the air in movements similar to those of the fantail. The intimidated explorer turned and set back out to sea.

When Tiwakawaka refused to tell his grandfather where fire was hidden on the island, Maui took the bird that meant so much to his grandson and squeezed it so hard that its eyes nearly popped out—hence the ocular prominence today. This also explains why the bird's tail projects so far behind its body and why it flies so erratically.

But the fantail got its revenge on Maui for the rough treatment when accompanying him on his last exploit to the realms of Hinenuitepo.

Hinenuitepo, goddess of night and of death, lived, as she does today, in the underworld of spirits. As mother of mankind, she decreed from the earliest days of creation that man should live one cycle of life, then die. Maui wanted to give mankind everlasting life. He sought to kill Hinenuitepo and thereby abolish death.

When Maui asked his father what Hinenuitepo looked like, the father replied: "You will see that her body is like that of a human being, but is of gigantic size, with thighs as red as the setting sun. You will see eyes of greenstone, flashing like the opening and shutting of the horizon in summer lightning. You will see teeth as sharp as flaked obsidian and a mouth like that of a barracuda, and hair like a tangled mass of sea kelp."

Maui chose several bird companions besides the fantail to accompany him on his great quest. Because he had the ability to change into many life forms, he was able to travel with these birds to the underworld as a sparrow hawk.

Maui's objective was to enter the womb of Hinenuitepo when she was sleeping and pass through her vital organs to her mouth, thus destroying death. He said to his companions, "My command is that when I enter the womb of Hinenuitepo, you must on no account move or make noise."

So Maui shape-shifted into the form of a worm and then entered the womb of the goddess of death. But as soon as he disappeared, the fantail began dancing with delight. Hinenuitepo was aroused with the commotion, felt the intruder, and closed her legs, strangling Maui, and the hope of immortality, to death.

Maurice draws the mythology around him like a warm blanket and then guides us to the modest home of his sister. Here we pass down a reception line rubbing noses with each relative, exchanging and intermingling the *ha*, the breath of life. Now, we are told, we are no long considered *manuhiris* (visitors), but rather we are *tangata whenua*, peoples of the land. This status comes with a price, however. For the rest of the stay, I am obliged to share in all the duties and responsibilities of the home people. In earlier times, this meant bearing arms in times of war or tending crops of *kūmara*, the sweet potato. Now I hope the obligation doesn't extend to washing dishes, my least-favorite chore. Kim, who inspires an irreproachable trust, goes on to lend a bit of the folklore behind the hongi. She says the gods created the first woman by molding her shape out of the earth. The god Tāne (a male) embraced the figure and breathed into the woman's nostrils. She then sneezed and made the first breath of life.

Maurice then takes us to a prehistoric *pa*, a fort that sits atop a bluff overlooking the bay at a place where there is no defense against the beauty. From this vantage, it seems you can see the curve of the earth.

Maurice sees a good future for New Zealand. "We made a lot of mistakes in the past. But our country has taken it upon itself to try and right the wrongs of our history, and that draws us even closer. We are ahead of the world in so many ways—not just with our environmental policies. As far as race relations, we lead the world."

I can't help but wonder if this is just Vaseline on the lens of a culture—if I am being subjected to some sort of magical thinking. Maurice and his family have investments in ancient bodies of knowledge whose relevance to our own time might be overestimated. Is this a dangerous book of ideas? Is this ethos real and germane? And if so, what is it about Māori that has allowed and galvanized this unified vision?

Maurice says the ethos is authentic and time-tested and that the Māori culture of storytelling has assured the continuance of key values and provided a spiritual security. And it is true that our minds come preloaded with mental cabinetry that makes information in the form of stories easier to retrieve than random files. With time, stories also undergo a kind of condensation, seeping into every texture of life, influencing thought and actions. And so Maurice illustrates with a story about the importance of code and protocol.

"Long ago, a man named Rata wished to fell a tree and hollow out a canoe so that he could make a voyage to avenge the death of his father. But he did not perform the necessary rituals, and the day after his tree had fallen he found it standing upright once more. Again Rata felled the tree, and again next day it was standing there. So he hid himself, and he discovered that the spirits of the forest had restored the tree to life because, as they told him, 'You did not consult us, so that we might know and consent to your cutting the neck of your ancestor Tāne.' The spirits then taught Rata the proper ceremonies, which Māori have performed ever since. Then, after Rata had done the right things, the spirits magically completed his task for him. In the morning the canoe lay finished in the forest."

With his Yodalike deportment, Maurice continues: "From the old stories we get our values. It's impossible to say to a Māori, 'Forget the past.' Our past is our present. Kaitiakitanga is our future."

"What is kaitiakitanga?" I ask.

As precise and elusive as a Basho haiku, he answers: "There is no English translation. Pakeha endorse it, but they don't know what it means. The best way to convey it is through music."

Then, almost as if by magic, Maurice produces a guitar and offers to sing the song his older sister wrote as a hymn for visiting Pakeha. We get both the Māori and the English versions: "Stand in the heart of the day. Gather round to you the essence of nature. Share with others and enjoy the beauty. Stand in the heart of the day." It was written in a day but seems a song with eternity authored in it.

The draft wafting up the palisade is cool, like the feel of new milk against a cheek. We inhale the air and look out to a sea on fire with the setting sun. It seems we can see to the borderline of forever. Then there is a point where the surface stars, and from it the water suddenly gushes in a plume of diamonds—a whale.

"The whales were once kaitiaki for us," Maurice says. "But then they were hunted for a long time, and Māori were as involved as anyone. They were almost hunted away. But now we are the kaitiaki for whales, and they are coming back."

A TIME
TO KRILL

Kia mōhio tika te tangata i ngā korero me ngā tikanga o te taiao.

The one who teaches about the environment must understand the structure, lore, and rituals pertaining to it.

The European settlement of Kaikoura began in 1842, when Scotsman Robert Fyffe established a whaling station. The operation employed a lot of local Māori men who were ready to forgo their traditional respectful relationship with whales for the opportunity to be employed in a relatively high-paying job.

Harpooned whales, mostly southern right whales, were dragged to a large rock shelf in the bay, where flesh was removed and boiled down for oil to lubricate the clanking wheels of the Industrial Revolution. Southern right whales were already rare in the 1840s, and their numbers soon collapsed. But it was crude oil as well as decreasing numbers that put a stake in the heart of the industry. Oil from the earth became so plentiful, so versatile, and so cheap that it quickly replaced whale oil in many applications.

Humpback and sperm whales sustained a small whaling industry in Kaikoura until the early twentieth century. Whales were still being hunted in other South Island locations until commercial whaling ended in New Zealand in 1964. In 1978, the Marine Mammals Protection Act was passed, providing protection to New Zealand's whales, dolphins, and seals.

In the bleed of early light, we make our way down Whaleway Road to the back of the old railway station, whose name has been changed to The Whaleway Station. There, at the Flukes Café, we meet Kauahi Ngapora, the gentle-eyed operations manager for Whale Watch, a Māori-owned ecotourism enterprise. Kauahi has worked with the company for fourteen years. His mother initially dragged him into it, and he at first resented the employment because he wanted to simply play, like most teens. Kauahi's first job was handing out spew buckets to the tourists; the owners couldn't afford sick bags. After a use, he'd rinse the bucket, then recirculate it.

"It's tail time!" A giant sperm whale, largest carnivore in the world, crashes through the skin of the sea and sends its fluke flying at the sky off the coast of Kaikoura.

"From a caregiver, I became a guide, which was a huge step up for me because Māori are very shy people. So talking to boatloads of people was for me very difficult, but I got the hang of it in the end. And then I had the opportunity to become a skipper. Which was another huge move for me. And I just progressed from there. I'm the operations manager now. I'm responsible for our clients from the time they walk in the door to when they leave."

At the marina we walk a gangplank onto *Te Ao Marama* ("The World of Enlightenment"), a sleek, custom-designed catamaran the color of a blue whale and propelled, like so many boats in New Zealand, by jet-ted water, which is not only quieter than traditional tour craft propulsion systems but also can't injure ocean mammals with propellers. Inside, the air-conditioned cabin is lined with gray whale-colored cushioned chairs that face a flat plasma monitor a quarter the size of the boat. The screen shows state-of-the-art graphics and animation describing the marine life and the underwater Kaikoura Canyon, an ancient river trench now flooded. New Zealand's longest river is under water.

Three miles wide and deeper than Arizona's Grand Canyon, the Hikurangi Trench is less than a mile off the coast, making it one of the few places in the world where the edge of the continental shelf is so close to land.

Two cultures crashed here; two oceans collide. These waters are the inflection point where two currents meet—one subtropical and the other subantarctic. As a result, the sea is hyperrich in nutrients, minerals, and floating plankton, which attracts huge numbers of whales, dolphins, and seals. Seven species of whales visit these waters, including the blue whale, the largest, heaviest, and loudest animal on Earth.

Out beyond the bay, above the great trench, the water turns dark green, and the sea looks empty, though deep below swarm millions of krill and other zooplankton. The skipper cuts the engine, and a crew member drops a hydrophone into the water. It picks up a trickle of submarine-like sonar clicks and echoes. To locate the whales, the crew uses a directional mike that picks up whale sounds. The crew avoids reproducing the sounds underwater because Māori believe that would interfere with the whales' tracking systems. We start the engine and chase the sounds.

Streaks of white paint the blue sky. New Zealand has the most diverse seabird community in the world. The snowy albatross glide lock-winged above the boat in a graceful waltz, sometimes swooping toward the surface, wings almost touching the sea, then catching an updraft and turning toward the sun. Their ten-foot wingspan is the greatest of any bird's in the world today. A nimbus of pelagic birds—seagulls, shags, terns, mollymawks, and petrels (named for Saint Peter, who sought to walk on water)—mingle as well, and the Māori interpreter barks an overly enthusiastic narration, as sincere as a mock news program; he would fit perfectly as a guide on a jungle-boat ride at Disney.

The hydrophone is again dropped over the side, but this time a welter of sounds spill forth: chirps, warbles, whistles, eerie shrieks, and long, keening notes. Several whales seem to be chatting, trading gossip, and telling stories of long journeys—or of humans who rode their backs.

Now it's just a matter of waiting. Whale Watch has a 95 percent success rate for seeing whales, and managers are so certain of a sighting they offer an 80 percent refund if a guest doesn't get at least a glimpse. We wait. The boat bobs, and Laura Hubber from the BBC, here doing a radio story on the whales, grabs a sickness bag and leans over the edge. The skipper moves the boat and listens. We wait some more. Diatoms of light rant and waver. The boat moves again. This is the "hunting" part of the expedition. A clean breeze feathers up as I lean over the rail, eyes sweeping the molten sea. Then a voice down deck shouts: "There, there, there!" A column of vapor and water spouts like a silver fountain. A raspy, whooshing sound pours across the bow.

Everyone points to what looks like a waxy, black iceberg drifting along the surface. Then suddenly there is a breach. "Thar she blows," the intercom squawks with all the shock of Tuna Surprise. It's tail time, Kauahi says, as the giant sperm whale, largest carnivore in the world, crashes through the skin of the sea and sends its fluke flying at the sky. What looks like a set of pterodactyl wings bends and seems to lyrically wave at us, then stands motionless for a moment on the surface of the sea. Finally, down the

One of the Whale Watch fleet, a sleek, custom-designed catamaran the color of a blue whale and propelled by jetted water.

tail plunges, a commanding movement made with amazing grace, the start of a deep dive. Then there is nothing but the horizon and a nettled circle of sea. Kauahi interprets some of what we see: "All he's doing up here is reoxygenating his system. Depending upon how deep he's headed, for every minute he's on the surface, he can manage five or six minutes below. He can dive over a mile in pursuit of prey, which includes krill and giant squid. He'll probably go down for forty to sixty minutes now. Good, isn't it?"

We're told the whale's name is Tiaki, short for "kaitiaki," guardian. He's about fifty tons (more than four African elephants) and almost sixty feet long (about the same as our vessel). The legends say that originally whales were the helpers of men lost at sea, as long as the humans knew how to speak the language of the sea. But as the world aged and men grew away from their roots in the sea, they began to lose the language and the power to interlock. Paikea did not lose the sacred speech, and when he asked his whale to bring him to the land far to the south, it was done.

For a long time, the descendants of Paikea always honored Tangaroa, the lord of the sea, by not taking more fish than needed to feed a family or community and by observing ceremonies of respect. Then came the moment when man turned on the great mammal that had been such a spiritual consort, and the whale killing and flensing began. Now the tables have turned again, and it is modern Māori, with their whale-watching concerns, who are acting as custodians of the whales.

It's impossible to witness a whale breaching here and not imagine riding the back of one of these creatures. The story of Paikea and the whale, so potently rendered in the book *The Whale Rider* and the Oscar-nominated film *Whale Rider,* espouses a spiritual bond between human beings and the natural world and suggests hope for a knitted, not disentangled, fabric of future history and teaching tales.

As we head back to shore, the sea around the boat crackles with a swarm of light. It is a pod of dusky dolphins. They make happy leaps and dances about the pressure waves of the boat, possessed of some sort of tarantism. They somersault and dart like silver dreams, and the children on board, I among them, shriek with delight. I fix my eyes on one sprinting about the bow, and it seems to catch my thoughts with its nose and makes a nodding motion back.

Once back in town—a long strip of backpacker bars, sports boutiques, galleries, hostels, cafes (featuring, of course, the local crayfish), and lots of imagery of whales—Kauahi, who has the build of a black pine and as such is quite persuasive without saying a word, makes an undeclinable suggestion that we try his favorite fish restaurant, The Green Dolphin. There I share my recollection that when I passed through Kaikoura twenty years ago it was a one-opossum town, hard to find on many maps, where the only coffee was instant. But now the town is one of the most popular tourist destinations in the whole of the country. What happened?

Kauahi looks out the window toward the sea as though looking into a living past. "In 1987, unemployment was the biggest growth industry in Kaikoura, followed closely by crime. The town was going down the tubes and almost entirely dependent on outside influences. I was only fifteen, but my family was unemployed. A group of local Māori took a very big risk: they had no business experience; tourism was a dirty word; they were unable to get financing from the banks. So four families mortgaged their houses to get the first boat."

Kaikoura is one of the few places in the world where whales can be sighted year-round. In the first season, Whale Watch carried about three thousand people. Today, the enterprise carries about one hundred thousand annually, and about a million visitors pass through town each year. Whale-watching contributes more than NZ$120 million annually to the New Zealand economy, and the bulk comes from Kaikoura. Māori see no borders between animals and men, but a political border offshore cuts the two like a knife. Just beyond the legal limits of New Zealand waters, whaling continues by countries that continue to claim killing rights to the animals. They ignore the rights of communities such as Kaikoura to engage in truly sustainable use. You can watch a whale many times, but you can kill it only once.

The modern Māori of Kaikoura have ridden the backs of their local whales to a new economic prosperity. Whale Watch is the largest employer in the community, consisting mostly of Kati Kuri, a subtribe of the Ngāi Tahu. Many of the families that fled during the hard times have returned. Māori from other tribes are coming for work and ideas. Whale Watch has become something of a metonymic model for indigenous peoples around the world. Australian aborigines, Native Americans, and Indian peoples have made pilgrimages here to learn how to start and manage a sustainable ecotourism enterprise. "This success gives us great pride," Kauahi says. "It ensures that what we saw today can be enjoyed by my children and my children's children."

And by the visitors as well. Many are from Japan, a nation that might be called the dark star of whaling, and yet the citizens who watch the whales are often moved to tears, and many believe that witnessing these creatures and their magic changes hearts and minds. "I've guided people who flew halfway round the world to come here and see whales," Kauahi says. "And when the first one surfaced, I watched as my guests broke down and cried. We made their dream come true. And I believe strongly that they take back these experiences into their lives.

"Māori from the early days have had a lot respect for the whales. We didn't hunt for them before Pakeha, but if a whale washed up on the beach, it was seen as a gift from the gods, and we received it for bone, for carving, for meat. The whales were once guardians for us.

"Today we see ourselves as the kaitiaki for the whales, looking after them for the tides of the future. Today our harpoons are cameras."

ADVENTURES WITH PORPOISE

Kua tu ki te pari o te rua kua puta mai he huru kē.

One who has stood on the threshold of the abyss now sprouts forth anew.

After leaving Whale Watch, I hike over a hill for a view and pass a marker commemorating the death of Thomas Brent Smith. No matter how deep the conviction about the lore, no matter how passionate the belief in the symbiotic nexus between man and whale, no matter how strong the power of mutual guardianship, sometimes life takes untidy turns. Sometimes things don't fit the cosmology.

Tom Smith was a fisherman, diver, and renowned whale rescuer. He was a Pakeha kaitiaki in that he was an active guardian, ready to help man or whale at a moment's notice. He was the guy to call if a whale was in trouble, and he believed whales understood when he tried to help them.

In 2001, Tom Smith was photographed freeing a humpback tangled in crayfish-pot ropes off the Kaikoura coast. The animal had been snagged as it was migrating north from Antarctica. After he freed the whale, he told the local newspaper: "I was pretty scared. The first thing I did was make eye contact with its dinner plate-sized eye. It let out a roar of distress. It started whistling as I started to cut the loop of rope from around its head. I dumped the scuba gear back on the boat and hopped back in to cut the other tangled rope from the tail. When it stopped moving, I approached. The whale dropped its head and raised its tail, waiting for me to do the cutting. They talk about how whales know you are going to help them—I believe it."

But in June 2003, Tom set out to help another forty-foot humpback whale trapped in crayfish-pot lines about a mile off Sharks Tooth Point on the South Bay side of the Kaikoura peninsula. Tom dove into the one-hundred-fifty-foot-deep water where the whale was entangled and spent about five minutes trying to cut the lines. Then suddenly the whale thrashed its giant tail, smacking Tom squarely on the head and sending him down

Tom Smith drowned trying to free a humpback tangled in crayfish-pot ropes off the Kaikoura coast.

into the depths. He drowned. He was thirty-eight, the father of three, and beloved in the community. The whale, which Tom had freed, swam away.

Despite the hammering undertow of tragedy, I realize that kaitiakitanga is a social construct rather than an object, like a whale, in the unmolested natural world. Kaitiakitanga is conceived; whales are found. If there were no human beings, there would still be whales, but there would be no kaitiakitanga. But this does not mean that whales are what they are apart from human needs, interests, and even ideas.

This night, Maurice Manawatu presides over a meeting in Kaikoura among local Māori and Pakeha debating what to do about the threatened Hector's dolphin, found only along New Zealand coasts and one of the smallest and rarest dolphins in the world. Named after Sir

Dolphins of New Zealand, threatened by fishing nets, ship propellers, and warming seas.

James Hector, the curator of the Colonial Museum in Wellington in the early years of the twentieth century, the shallow-water cetaceans have had a tough go in recent years, not just from entanglement in fishermen's gill nets, but also from the propellers of boats—sometimes boats carrying tourists. It is a near-perfect illustration of the tragedy of the commons, the social trap that involves a conflict over resources between individual interests and the common good—the structural tension between free access to and unrestricted demand for a finite resource. Aristotle presaged it: "For that which is common to the greatest number has the least care bestowed upon it."

The best guess is that there are about seven thousand Hector's dolphins left, and the population is in decline. The World Wildlife Fund for

Nature as well as New Zealand's Department of Conservation have advocated creating a reserve that would prohibit fishermen from the waters, and the meeting tonight is to see whether a consensus might be reached on how to manage the resource locally rather than allow outsiders to steer its fate.

The meeting goes well. Pakeha and Māori, commercial fisherman and tourism entrepreneurs, boaters and divers, all agree that the Māori concept of limited and judicious use should be endorsed.

Lynda Kitchingham, representing the Royal Forest and Bird Protection Society (the largest nongovernment environmental group in New Zealand, now in its eighty-fifth year of operation, with branches throughout the country), volunteers her assessment after the meeting:

"We've been dealing with the issue of the Hector's dolphin, whose population has been decimated in the last thirty years. I wouldn't have believed this: we just about got a unanimous vote to come up with a protection policy by the end of the year, an almost total set-net ban along this coast for a temporary period. Even the fishermen agreed.

"The Forest and Bird Society put together a proposal for a small marine reserve on the peninsula, but we backed off that idea of permanence. We agreed to a Māori-style protection, meaning we don't close up an area forever, but only for a spell, and then reassess, and perhaps move the closure to another area."

Lynda is referring to the traditional Māori management technique called *rāhui,* which involves cordoning off a section of the sea and banning collection of any marine life in the area for a time while it restocks itself. It is, she says, a thread in the tapestry of kaitiakitanga.

"What I've come to see today is the importance of compromise," she says. "The hard-line environmental approach leaves too many people out. It's too radical. You have to keep the vision, but know that it's going to take time, take steps, and take compromise."

Another at the meeting is Māori elder Darcia Solomon, a woman who refuses to be marooned by age. Every Māori seems to have a different interpretation of kaitiakitanga. Or perhaps there is some conspiracy for each to release to inquiring Pakeha just a bead of this chainless necklace.

"I believe it is us," Darcia says. "We are the environment. That's what it means. It's about the next generation. It's about how we perform, and if we're not performing properly, the environment lets us know. I think we are the kaitiakitanga.

"My husband was a crab fisherman, and I fished with him for a year. The Hector's dolphins used to be there waiting for us, waiting for the boat, and they'd follow us around while we picked the pots up. And then follow us back to the point when we were going home. We believed they were our kaitiakis.

"We were all part and parcel in depleting the dolphins. We all need to own up to that and work together to protect them. Fishermen have to compromise to protect them; Māori have to compromise; and the government too. I don't believe this should be in the political arena. I believe communities should be looking after our foreshore. We shouldn't legislate natural things. We eat from the sea; we live from it.

"Now we should be looking after the dolphins. They don't hurt anybody. They're absolutely beautiful, and we should be looking after them like they looked after us."

The man in the room who has the most intimate link with the sea is Dick Kleel, a commercial set-netter and lobster fisherman for more than thirty years. He rather modestly considers himself to have "a good knowledge of the local fishery." He and some of his fisher colleagues have participated in research and believe they have the most accurate information about the condition of marine stocks. He also thinks, despite his own best efforts, that there is not enough research and data for anyone to make long-term decisions at this point. "There's been only a limited amount of research done—in my opinion, not enough to actually go with total bans. We need to work together and find consensus for fishing in the area, to understand how the fisherman works, where the dolphin lives, where it's feeding, and work to a solution from there."

In this crowd it is Dick who has the most to lose if a total ban were imposed. Yet many are impressed with his efforts to find a solution that meets the needs of everyone, including the fish.

"I think eyes were opened quite a bit with this process," he says. "People realized that fishermen here aren't all the bad guys. We're conservationists at heart ourselves. We don't want to see the dolphin disappear; it's of no value to us.

"So the biggest thing is looking after what we've got and trying to do it better—so there will still be fish in the future."

Also in attendance is Department of Conservation marine specialist Andrew Baxter, who credits the Māori community for calling for a more comprehensive look at the issues. He admits that a reserve or permanent closure is too simplistic and inadequate.

"We've been trying to identify and find consensus on how the coast is used, agreeing on intrinsic spiritual, cultural, commercial, and recreational values," Andrew says. "The next crucial steps will be identifying the threats to those values and coming up with solutions as a community.

"It's never easy. If everything were black and white, if there were a simple solution, we wouldn't have to be around this table at all, would we? People have to give something up to gain something—gives and gains. The government works with community groups all the time, but this might be one of the first where we've gathered a range of different interests into one group. This is kind of new, but seems to be gelling, and I could imagine it being used more around New Zealand in the future."

Lynda Kitchingham sums up the feelings as the meeting closes: "To be honest, I've been blown away by what we experienced today."

This kaka, or bush parrot, is among the varied birdlife on Kapiti Island.

LIKE NOTHING BUT ITSELF

Titiro atu tō kanohi ki Tairāwhiti ana, tēra whiti te rā kite ataata ka hinga ki muri i a koe.

Turn your face to the sun and the shadows fall behind you.

After bedding in the hundred-year-old Kincaid Lodge on a sheep and cattle farm originally owned by the whaler George Fyffe—the homestead is one of the many tourism spin-offs from the success of the whale-watching business—we head up the road to the local winery. The tasting room sits atop a limestone bluff with a selcouth view of the blue-green bay on one side, white peaks on the other. Clouds seem to hang motionless here, each a replica of the other, puffed and piled on a level base.

We spend the shank of the afternoon nibbling at cheese and sipping a selection of local wines, including the liquid franca of choice, a Tohu Pinot Noir from a nearby Māori vintner (medium garnet in color, the nose a mix of dark berries with some subtle, spicy oak). The signature wine is produced from free-draining native soils in four hectares surrounding the room and is crafted with sustainability in mind. The winery's owner is an enthusiastic patron of local arts and hosts an annual Recyclable Art fashion show in the spirit of the eco-theme of the whole of the community.

Over a glass of Noble One Late Harvest (a Riesling–Sauvignon Blanc blend with aromas of fig, ginger, honey, and apricot), the second-term mayor of Kaikoura, Kevin Heays, wanders in and cadges a sip. He's one of a handful of mayors throughout the world who endorsed the joint statement on achieving a nuclear-weapons-free world crafted by the Parliamentary Network for Nuclear Disarmament.

Kevin has been in the district twenty-three years and witnessed the transformation of Kaikoura from back shadow to main attraction. By his reckoning, Kaikoura was once the kind of place visited as a prophylaxis to hope and romance. He uncorks his memory:

The trees are alive with spirits in Aotearoa.

"When I was a boy, you stopped here, if you had to, for some fish-and-chips—then you got out, fast." Now he calls the place "Paradise, New Zealand," and reels off all the eco-friendly attractions, from bird-watching to horseback riding to wine tasting. Then I notice a round pin on his lapel and lean in to peer at its green logo of the earth with a checkmark across its face. The mayor says it is from Green Globe, the United Kingdom–based tourism-and-travel-industry auditor that offers benchmarking for responsible behavior across the bottom lines of economic, social, and environmental management.

"Yes, we're the first local authority in the world to be benchmarked as a Green Globe community, back in 2002," Kevin says. "Hotels and tour operators have been accredited by Green Globe, but we're the first living community. It gives us a framework to be watchdogs for ourselves, to make sure we're not wrecking the place. But it's also good business."

Kaikoura, the mayor says, decided to focus on waste management. "Because it's so small and pristine, waste was clearly going to be a humongous problem.

"As tourism grew, thanks to the Māori whale-watch tours, it was evident something had to be done. The local landfill, a traditional Kiwi hole in the ground, had only a few years left before it would be full. We wouldn't be allowed to create another hole, which meant the expensive prospect of shipping refuse out.

"So we focused on recycling and reuse. Luckily, the Kaikoura community knows that without a clean, green, pristine environment, we're going to lose our visitors. If we lose our visitors, we lose our district. We're now aiming for a 100 percent landfill diversion rate. We now have 97 percent of residents recycling, which is amazing. We have a 58 percent diversion rate. A new scheme starting soon, ZORG—Zero Organic Waste—will bring us up to 95 percent diversion from our hole in the ground."

I ask if the mayor has followed Prime Minister Helen Clark's proposals to make the whole country carbon neutral.

"As soon as we heard about it, we wrote to her the next day, inviting her down here to have a look around and use this place as an example of what other districts should be doing. She's very keen to do that, and we're looking forward to the visit."

That seems a good idea. I ask if she has scheduled a visit yet.

"No. She's a very busy lady." He laughs. "She has a country to run."

I ask how an entire community becomes benchmarked.

The mayor explains that to become certified, the community first had to measure its environmental impact, calculating how much energy was used in a year, how much greenhouse gases and waste were produced, what proportion of the land was native vegetation, what percentage of herbicides and pesticides was biodegradable, how clean the water was, even how many road accidents involved chemical spills (one). For instance, from July 2003 through June 2004, each person in Kaikoura (including tourists) used enough energy to power thirty-two one-hundred-watt lightbulbs for a year (103 gigajoules of energy each). To offset the carbon dioxide emissions produced by this, each person would need to plant 467 trees. Of course, every person and every business uses energy; all create carbon dioxide and other waste—and each can reduce impact. But to start, there has to be a baseline.

Once benchmarked, residents, visitors, and businesses can manage and reduce effects by adopting policies and practices that lead toward sustainability, or to an even better place: betterment, which the mayor says is his goal.

"Even the Kaikoura Winery has been benchmarked," Kevin Heays offers in a seeming state of ataraxia. He raises a glass of 2006 (off-dry) Riesling (pale yellow with orange, honey, pear, and white-water aromas; a fruit-forward palate with a baiser of ginger spice that finishes clean) and clinks our glasses in an eco-toast: "When good wine is fixed with great natural beauty, happiness cannot be augmented, either by more accomplishments or by a longer life." And so it goes.

THE PRICE OF EMISSIONS

Kohikohia he kai nō tō māra, ka hoatu ai i tētahi wahanga.

Gather food from your garden, and give some of it away.

Feeling the tightness in my hair shirt of guilt about my own carbon contributions as I travel around New Zealand, I next head over to another Kaikoura operation taking root: Trees for Travellers. Trees, of course, are natural carbon sinks that suck the carbon out of the atmosphere and give back oxygen, an action that in sufficient volume could stop or reverse harmful climate change.

Climate change is a natural process. Greenhouse gases, such as carbon dioxide and methane, trap the sun's heat inside the earth's atmosphere. For the past one hundred fifty years or so, humankind has been adding greenhouse gases to the atmosphere at an increasing rate by burning fossil fuels such as coal and oil, stamping the wrinkle deeper on the brow of our earth.

The extra gas is combining with what's already present to make greenhouse-gas levels the highest in history, in the process heating the planet. As of this writing, the number of Category 4 and 5 hurricanes has almost doubled in the past thirty years, and at least 279 species are moving their habitats closer to the poles to get away from the increasing heat of the equator.

If temperatures continue to increase, the results could be catastrophic; some credibly predict that deaths from global warming will double in twenty-five years—to three hundred thousand people a year. As Nobel Peace Prize winner Al Gore showed so graphically in his slide show–movie, with the loss of shelf ice in Greenland and Antarctica, sea levels could rise more than twenty feet, devastating coastal areas worldwide.

Heat waves would become more frequent and intense; droughts and wildfires would occur more often. The Arctic Ocean could be ice-free in summer, and more than a million species worldwide could be extinct by 2050, making the earth as sapless as a mumbled bone.

Unprepossessingly headquartered at the city landfill, the Trees for Travellers operation is part of a nonprofit organization called Innovative Waste Kaikoura (majority-owned by Kaikoura Wastebusters) that hopes to achieve zero waste by 2015. I meet with Steve Gill, a scruffy lad whose sweater hangs down over dirt-grimed jeans like the tongue of a sheepdog. He calls himself "The Tree Guy."

Steve first shows me around the nursery, where native trees donated by locals for the program are prepared. There are yellow bellflowers, cabbage trees, and akeakes, a Māori name that means "forever and ever," referring to the amazing hardness of the wood. Akeakes are the preferred trees for walking sticks and the power staffs of chiefs. Steve fondly fingers another branch and says, "I had a dream about this tree. The dream said to me, 'The ngaio is king,' which makes sense as you can plant it anywhere, and it is a nursing tree, helping others to grow. I have very good feelings about this tree."

Trees may in fact be the methadone for the planet's carbon addiction, and New Zealand has a lot of room to plant. Trees for Travellers is a proactive part of the benchmarking for the Kaikoura community. Steve says the auditors have calculated that neutralizing the carbon emissions of the travelers who come to Kaikoura will require the planting of about a million trees. The program has planted one thousand two hundred to date.

So I do my part and buy a sapling, a kauri, the native conifer that grows biggest and oldest in New Zealand. It is the tree that was almost cut to extinction during the height of the boatbuilding boom. What is the price of emission? I pay NZ$20, and Steve hands me the yard-high sprout, with its base wrapped in a plastic bag.

Steve then takes me to a grassy knoll on a council reserve that he personally cleared of gorse, the invasive weed that European settlers introduced as sheep feed but which now has taken over much of the land. Charles Darwin, visiting New Zealand in December 1835, noted the presence of gorse hedges and observed:

"In many places I noticed several sorts of weeds, which, like the rats, I was forced to own as countrymen. A leek has overrun whole districts, and will prove very troublesome, but it was imported as a favour by a French vessel. The common dock is also widely disseminated, and will, I fear, for ever remain a proof of the rascality of an Englishman, who sold the seeds for those of the tobacco plant."

Steve is pleased to have rid the hill of gorse. "We're reintroducing native trees with this program. I'm most excited about reforestation." But perhaps concerned he may not have sufficiently overegged the pudding, he goes on to point out the added benefits of newly planted native trees: attracting native birdlife, preventing erosion, and helping with local employment.

We pick out a spot that enjoys a grand view of the sea. "This is a nice neighborhood," Steve says with a grin. "Your tree will be very happy here. I'll even bring him blankets on cold nights."

Steve hands me a shovel, and I start to dig my heart out. I've done a lot of traveling, and so I figure I owe a lot of trees, but a kauri is a good start. It could live for thousands of years. "Your grandchildren's grandchildren can travel back to earth to visit your tree," Steve says, smiling like a hammock hooked to high branches. Each tree is identified with GPS coordinates and a unique number so purchasers don't have to fly back to New Zealand to check on their trees. They can do the checkup online. (The

GPS coordinates for my tree are 2566300 east and 5865888 north; if you go to the Trees for Travellers Web site, treesfortravellers.co.nz, and key in my tag number, 1477, you can see how my little kauri is doing.) Though the program is just four years young, travelers have bought trees for all sorts of occasions and honorings, from weddings to births of children to business deals and deaths. One traveler even stipulated that his own ashes be spread at the base of his tree. (At this writing he is still alive and less guilty.)

I dig a hole about two feet deep, then, with instructions from Steve, loosen the clay so the roots won't have to work too hard, and decant a layer of rocks into the bottom. Then we pour in topsoil, clay, and composted soil, compounded from Steve's recipe and much of it from the Innovative Waste landfill. At last we remove the tree from its bag, loosen its roots, and feed it to the earth.

"I feel less guilty already," I proffer.

I give my personal carbon sink a good watering, then step back to admire its new home. "I can feel the scales tipping back the right way."

Steve then stamps the soil. "I would say that whenever the pace of your life leaves you feeling a little disconnected, think of your tree." And I do.

Linda Pharazyn of Fyffe View Ranch says, "There is nothing neater than riding through water on a horse."

NOT LESS THAN THAN EVERYTHING

Ngā whetū huihui i te rangi
Ko tātou ka whakarautia.

Behold the firmament of glistening stars
We linger leisurely and wonder.

New Zealand does not suffer from lack of adventures, and so before leaving Kaikoura I follow a recommendation from Mayor Kevin Heays to sample another offering: horseback riding at the four-hundred-acre Fyffe View Ranch, owned and operated by Linda and Simon Pharazyn.

Mounting a standardbred named Doc, I head out with Ian and Linda alongside, clopping along a mosaic of nodding greensward and burnished stone, crooking through copses of native trees, and coiling softly into fern forests. I gaze in all directions and enter pure imagination, the wondrous worlds of childhood cowboy fancy. This part of New Zealand seems a place too far, too bucolic to ever breathe in life outside the mind; yet here it is, a living mural of wild hills and bending light. It is a kind of faith come to life.

Linda and her husband felt the same thing when they moved here from the North Island three years ago. "When you stand on our deck and look to the left—stunning mountains covered in snow—then to the right—aquamarine blue sea stretching for miles—what more can I say? Though it took four years to find a property that caught our hearts and made us feel we were coming home as we drove up the drive. We have no regrets at the move, no intention to move on."

As we proceed in a leisurely gait down a dappled path, Linda points at the rows of kanuka and manuka trees (manuka honey is the Champagne of honeys) and tells how Captain Cook's sailors used tea made from the leaves of these trees to fight scurvy. Today they are commonly called tea (or ti) trees. "This is where we get our tea-tree oil from. The tea is very astringent so not very popular, though the backcountry stockman or keen hunter will still make a billy of it around the campfire.

Tea-tree oil collected on the east coast of New Zealand has incredibly high antiseptic properties and has been proven to work against several modern-day afflictions that are proving difficult to handle with prescription antibiotics. Unfortunately, as our tea tree oil is so readily available, there is no option to patent the product, so big pharmaceuticals make more money out of their less-effective synthetic products."

We pass through a clearing, golden with ripe grass. Everything seems different at this pace. Movement seems charged with sublimity, danger, and grace. An intense light reigns over the hills, a light that seems to clarify distances. The mountains are crowned with a silvery radiance which melts into shadowy ravines. Everything—hills, woods, ancient rocks— floats in chasms of blue air. Clouds drift imperceptibly above the valley. It's easy to imagine we are riding through a ghost of a world, a lost world.

Traveling this way, I regret the invention of the car. Until, that is, we come to a steep decline that spills into the rushing Kowhai River. Ian and Linda, both veteran equestrians, have no problem steering their steeds down the path, but I can't get Doc to budge. He bucks his head, stomps his front legs, and pulls sideways, and I try in vain to reign him in. "You're rattling his dags," Ian suggests.

"What?"

"Dags are dingleberries, the little pieces of shit that get stuck in sheep hair. They rattle when a sheep gets anxious."

"You'll be right," Linda offers with a smile that could make sunburn. "Just be firm." But no matter how firm I pretend to be, Doc has his own agenda, until Linda steps back up the trail and gives Doc a kick in the pants. Then in a minute we're splashing across the stream, which glitters as it spills over stones and captures the sun's glint, and Linda seems a woman in uncontaminated content. "There is nothing neater than riding through water on a horse."

Back at the stables, I can't resist asking Linda if, as Pakehas living in Kaikoura, she and her family endorse and practice kaitiakitanga.

"Yes, definitely, we regard ourselves as temporary guardians of our land, ensuring its lasting future for tomorrow's children. We have a large expanse of native bush at the back of our property running up into Mount Fyffe, which we are vigorously protecting to ensure the regenerating native bush can be enjoyed for generations to come."

It's time to jaunt north again, so I tip my hat to Linda and her family and the ranch hands, and join Ian in the rental car. Up the coast we drive, powered by curiosity. In spite of past travesties—and Ian is not shy about citing them—there does seem here today an enlightened recognition of the potent values intrinsic to the country's cultural, spiritual, and ecological well-being. It seems to run deep in the blood.

From Kaikoura, the highway edges up a narrow coastal road between the sheer, snow-dusted Kaikoura Ranges and slate-gray pebble beaches where fur seals bask at the brim of an ocean smoothed like a sheet to the end of the sky. New Zealand fur seals were hunted to near extinction in the nineteenth century for their skins (it was in vogue for a time in London to wear seal-fur hats), but, now protected, they thrive along this coast. I stare out the car window at the seals; they look like well-done sausages scattered in a scene. Some frolic in the water. Some slump on the rocks, sometimes fanning their whiskers, as though meditating or caught in a dream. As the drive continues, dark clouds swim overhead like a pod of whales.

Understanding is accumulated, like sediment, and some layers may be inaccessible to even the most determined. No matter how much

Riding at the four-hundred-acre Fyffe View Ranch.
Everything seems different at this pace. Movement seems
charged with sublimity, danger, and grace.

I spade and grub, I will always be an arriviste in this land, my appreciation of the culture imperfect. It is a basic tenet of Māoridom that sacred knowledge is not to be shared with the *tutua*, or the common herd, lest such knowledge be mishandled or abused. Telluric wisdom, guidelines, and protocols are to be shared only with select aspirants who after long tutelages and many trials are deemed fit to hold such profound knowledge.

But I do believe that kaitiakitanga can be described with a portmanteau: *chaordic,* invented by Dee Hock, founding CEO of VISA, the credit-card company. He says the word refers to "complex systems that blend order and chaos."

It sounds like a Marlborough wine. I stop in the region's capital, Blenheim, in the area known as "Top of the South" (the northernmost sector of the South Island) for a sip of the famously crisp Sauvignon Blanc. There was a time when the world response to New Zealand wine was a twist on Dorothy Parker's chiasmus: "I'd rather have a frontal lobotomy than a bottle in front of me." But that began to change in the 1970s, and today some critics rank several New Zealand wines as among the world's finest. A swirl and a sip, though, and the memories flow.

THERE'S A FJORD IN YOUR FUTURE

Kia mate ururoa, kei mate wheke.

It is better to fight and die like a shark than to give in like an octopus.

I n the late 1990s, I found myself immersed in Marlborough country by chance, having given a presentation at a tourism conference. With a couple of extra days available, I decided to take the opportunity to look around. Because it has almost a thousand miles of coastline (20 percent of New Zealand's entire shores) and some high mountains, scooping valleys, and rushing rivers, it seemed a place I would enjoy. I had never heard of kaitiakitanga, nor do I believe that many non-Māori had made its acquaintance at that point, but the place was beyond the quotidian sphere in its wilderness integrity. The people of this region intuitively knew to be shepherds to the undefiled works of nature.

I joined David Watson, owner of Marlborough Sounds Adventure Company, who had relocated to Marlborough after half a career leading adventures in Australia. We hopped an early morning water taxi from the ferry terminal at Picton Harbor and rode up a long, crooked finger of an ocean-drowned river valley into a maritime maze. Captain James Cook is credited with being the first European to sail into the Marlborough Sounds in January 1770. After months at sea, both men and ship were weary. He anchored at what he named Ship's Cove, a respite tucked away from the elements. It provided freshwater and waves of coastal forest woods that he used for repairs, as well as scurvy grass, a cure for the vitamin C deficiency from which his men suffered. He returned four more times during his explorations of the South Pacific, spending more than one hundred days in the refuge of the cove. While Cook was making his repairs, his onboard botanist, Joseph Banks, recorded seeing a bird with a burnt-orange back, a bird that would be named the South Island saddleback. I looked around as David readied the fiberglass kayaks and saw no bird of such coloration; it became extinct on the mainland by the beginning of the twentieth century.

Within the hour we slipped into the sea kayaks, pushed off from the crunchy beach into blue-green water, and paddled across the strait to Motuara Island, the wildlife sanctuary in the outer Queen Charlotte Sound. A twenty-minute walk from the jetty took us to Cook's Cairn, a monument marking the day the captain claimed the surrounding land for King George III and named the sheltered sound after the king's consort, Queen Charlotte Sophia. As we walked the corkscrew path to the island summit, we heard the silvery, ringing choruses of bellbirds and the chatter of fantails and bush robins, and passed a bird with a burnt-orange saddle and wattle. It was the rare South Island saddleback, which was reflourishing on this bubblelike isle, with some eighty now residing. Hopes are that they can be reintroduced to the mainland in the not-too-distant future. Also on the island (but they eluded us) were the Okarito brown kiwi, the Marlborough green gecko, and the Maud Island frog, all being recolonized and nurtured back into forming real populations. This amphibian hope gives me a personal charge. When I was quite young—maybe four or five—I was visiting my grandmother in Mount Carmel, Connecticut, and while playing out back I pulled a frog from its pond and put it in an abandoned bathtub. It tried to jump out but kept sliding back down the smooth porcelain in an endless loop. It seemed miserable, and so I picked it up to release it back into the woods. But it squirmed, and I held it too tightly—so tightly that suddenly its guts squeezed out its mouth, and it was dead. A part of me thinks that I have spent much of my life trying to reverse this crime, and that celebrating such places as this is a form of atonement.

We next climbed a platform and drank in a 360-degree panorama, watching the salty light sparkle off the Cook Strait like broken stars spilled into the sea. If there is a place in this sound that sounds the way

The shore at Motuara Island, the wildlife sanctuary in the outer Queen Charlotte Sound

the crew of the *Endeavour* must have heard it, then it must be here. Joseph Banks, when the vessel was anchored nearby, wrote: "This morn I was awakd by the singing of the birds ashore from whence we are distant not a quarter of a mile.... Their voices were certainly the most melodious wild musick I have ever heard, almost imitating small bells but with the most tuneable silver sound imaginable."

Cook's encounters with New Zealand were generally benign, though he lost ten sailors to the cooking pot. But by and large, Māori liked him, and he them. "Notwithstanding they are cannibals," Cook wrote, "they are naturally of a good disposition." Others in his wake fared worse. Marc-Joseph Marion du Fresne of France landed in 1772 at the Bay of Islands, where he and twenty-six of his crew members were killed by local Māori. Julien Crozet, who then led a punitive expedition that would kill some three hundred Māori, wrote, "There is amongst all the animals of creation none

127

There was a time when the world response to New Zealand wine was a twist on Dorothy Parker's chiasmus: "I'd rather have a frontal lobotomy than a bottle in front of me." But that began to change in the 1970s, and today some critics rank several New Zealand wines as among the world's finest.

more ferocious and dangerous for human beings than the primitive and savage man" of New Zealand. Māori were indisputably fierce warriors, cannibals, and slavers, and their assertiveness garnered a certain respect that survives today.

Back at the dock, we wormed into our kayaks and rotored off around Resolution Bay toward Endeavour Inlet, named for Cook's flat-bottomed former collier, which had carried him around the world. As we skidded by the cliffs, following in the paddle strokes of Kupe, the legendary Māori warrior, we passed little blue penguins and king cormorants, swooping terns and shearwaters, shags standing like statues, diving gannets, and white herons pausing on their way north to a particular pōhutukawa tree.

On the seam of water and shore, we glided by a sun-basking colony of New Zealand fur seals, looking like little old bald-headed ghosts playing among the bull kelp. We twirled through a labyrinthine fretwork of coves, bights, inlets, reaches, and runs. I couldn't help but appreciate the beauty of the clean lines the boat carved in the water as I spun my double blades like windmills. And, when I looked upward, beyond the banks, I saw a jag of dark mountains looking like an enormous green animal in repose. Tiritiri o te Moana, "gift of the sea," is what Kupe called this place when he paddled back to Hawaiki and told of his cool sea discovery.

Once at the Punga Cove Resort, then operated by refugee California wine-country innkeepers Lisa and George Smith, we berthed our boats at a little beach littered with sun-bleached shells and thick with the smell of brine. We walked a frilly trail up to our chalet and tucked into a spacious room with a view of calm water that glistened like distant paddles flashing. It was easy, and still is, to understand why my friend Tom Peirce and his father loved this country so much, making biannual treks all the way from Aspen.

The following morning dawned with ideal weather—hot, but not sultry; bright, but not glaring. We took off to tramp the Queen Charlotte Track. Unlike the famous Milford Track to the south, which requires advance bookings and is never an isolated experience, the Queen Charlotte Track is relatively unknown, with few trampers, though it is no less handsome. The track, forty-two miles long, is based on a series of bridle paths hewn by fin de siècle pioneers to connect the isolated farms of the sound. It wends its way past lush coastal forest, through groves of kamahi, beneath rata vines, around pristine bays, through farmland, and across skyline ridges.

At Punga Cove, we were starting the track about a third of the way through its course, having kayaked around from its start at Ship

Cove. Immediately, though, we shambled deep into the bush, brushing by sweet-smelling beech and moseying beneath New Zealand's only native palm, the feather-duster-shaped nikau, which means, I was told, "no nuts." (I was advised never to call a male New Zealander a nikau.) We tramped by the straight and digni-fied rimu, dripping with velvety folds of mosses and star-shaped ferns, perches for the chattering fantails, silvereyes, tomtits, gray warblers, kereu, and shin-ing cuckoos. At our feet, we twined past red supplejack berries, green hooded or-chids, and the creamy white flowers of the native clema-tis. Every now and then we would stop to soak in the scenery, which was almost painterly, like the watercol-ors I had seen of Captain Cook's anchorages. At appropriate intervals, we would boil the billy for tea and munch on yummy,

Of the twelve species of Metrosideros endemic to New Zealand, half are either climbers or epiphytes. The northern rata germinates as an epiphyte in the branches of a host tree, colonizing the trunk as it sends it roots to the ground.

homemade ANZAC biscuits, baked by David's wife, Sara Archdale, rea-son enough to travel ten thousand miles. Then we were off again down

130

the track, the afternoon light shafting through the moss-strung forest as though from a motivational poster.

After a full day of bush walking, we reached Portage, a saddle where Māori once hauled their wakas between the Queen Charlotte and Kenepuru sounds. Here we caught a water taxi to the Raetihi Lodge, nestled on the edge of the Kenepuru Sound, run by world travelers and collectors Lyn and Roger Jarvis. Theirs was a museum of assorted tastes, including everything from Japanese gardens to New Guinean carvings, from English antiques to Bornean tribal art, from Turkish rugs to African skins, a place out of Ripley's Believe It or Not! and a somewhat hallucinogenic contrast to the wilderness around us, further enhancing the wonderland qualities of the region. It was also telling that, having circumnavigated the globe, the Jarvises decided the finest piece of real estate at which to hang their art and hats was in Marlborough.

The day following, we took off mountain biking the remainder of the Queen Charlotte Track, down a fairy-tale section that could be the inspiration for Middle-earth. In fact, not far from here, New Line Cinema and director Peter Jackson were filming the first installment in J. R. R. Tolkien's *Lord of the Rings* trilogy, a set of movies that would do more to promote New Zealand as a destination than anything before or since, though more and more films keep trying.

On fat tires, we wound beneath leafy branches that hung like waterfalls, past stands of magical trees, such as kamahi, manuka, and mahoe; tall, black fern trees called mamaku; the unloved gorse; kanuka, introduced into New Zealand for fencing in the 1840s; and the broad leaves of five finger. We pumped up to undulating ridges where we could gaze down on the Pelorus Sound, which was dotted with black buoys marking mussel farms growing the famous green-lipped mussels. And then, after riding above Mistletoe Bay, the track sidled along a viridian hill, skirting some farm paddocks, and dropped into Davis Bay, where it widened and flattened for a final roll at water level through a beech forest and into Anakiwa, the end of the road.

To cap off the four-day expedition, I went road biking and wine tasting with local adventure guru Wally "The Wonderman" Bruce, who spent years guiding in Europe and North America but circled back to Marlborough to put down roots. We pedaled the Queen Charlotte Drive to the hamlet of Havelock, an old gold-mining village on the Pelorus Sound which once offered twenty-three hotels for those flocking in with the fever. Now it is an out-of-the way stop better known for its mollusks than its mining. We ordered a pot of fresh, fat steamers and a plump platter of grilled flats at the Mussel Boys Restaurant, "The Greenshell Mussel Capital of the World."

Then it was up the wine trail to the Wairau Valley, the Napa Valley of the antipodes. Marlborough has quietly become an award-winning wine producer in the last few years. The four thousand acres of vineyards have stony, free-draining soils with abundant, pure underground water. Coupled with Marlborough's long, dry summers and cool autumns, that provides a recipe for the production of grapes of high quality and intense flavors. Our first stop was Wairau River Wines, a one hundred twenty-hectare vineyard on the banks of the Wairau River. We sipped a 1998 Sauvignon Blanc, fermented in five-year-old French oak barrels; a creamy 1996 Chardonnay; and a lime- and marmalade-flavored 1998 Botrytised Riesling. Then we moseyed over to the Grove Mill Winery, where we sampled a straw-green 1997 Sauvignon Blanc, crisp and clean, as fine as any I've tasted in Burgundy. And our final taste was a 1997 Reserve Gewürztraminer, with an aroma and taste of lychee and spice.

The day and the trip were capped at the Hotel d'Urville, a ten-room boutique hotel in a converted neoclassic bank building in downtown Blenheim. Named for the French explorer Dumont d'Urville, who charted some of the fjords of the Marlborough Sounds, it seemed the fitting place to end my own little voyage of discovery. I joined owners Chris and Julia Knowles at their big, curving wooden bar in the shape of a ship's bow, surrounded by maps and charts of early New Zealand, and listened to them tell tales of adventuring in Africa and around the world for twenty years. After they'd seen and done it all, they decided that Marlborough was the premium place on the planet, the place to pitch their permanent tent. We ordered some pâté and garlic-steamed mussels and a bottle of Marlborough's *méthode champenoise* sparkling wine, and raised

a glass to adventure and the address they called home.

At this point, back to the present, I have a choice in ways to cross the Cook Strait, one of the most dangerous stretches of water in the world, to get to the North Island: take the ferry, take a puddle hopper of a flight, or try another adventure, which is a commercial offering to skydive into Wellington. It's a blustery day; the wind is yowling. So I take the commuter flight.

The New Zealand nikau is the world's most southerly-growing palm.

WHEELS OF FORTUNE

Kaua e hoki i te waewae tūtuki, ā, pā anō mā te ūpoko pakaru.

Do not turn back because of a stumbling of the feet, but only because of a broken head.

The author stooping to an icy reception in the Franz Josef Glacier

photo courtesy of Laura Hubber

Tree conservationist Stephen King. Stephen made a name for himself in the 1970s when he squatted high up in a giant tōtara tree in the Pureora Forest in protest against the logging of native woodlands. He dared the bulldozers to advance and won. The government ordered the felling stopped.

photo courtesy of Didrik Johnck

Inside the sweeping entrance of Te Papa, meant to be a waharoa, or gateway. Inside are five floors of taonga, art, artifacts, weapons, and stories. Around everything is an epidermis of narrative by which the world is rendered intelligible.

The author rowing the rapids with his son, Walker Bangs, in the bow

photo courtesy of Walker Bangs

New Zealand Prime Minister Helen Clark

photo courtesy of Tourism New Zealand

Richard and Steve Grill from Trees for Travellers

photo courtesy of Small World Productions

The dusky dolphins of Kaikoura. They make happy leaps and dances about the pressure waves of the boat, possessed of some sort of tarantism. They somersault and dart like silver dreams.

photo courtesy of Didrik Johnck

On the Class V Kaituna River, a sprint of a watercourse that spins near the boiling mud pools and hell-like geysers of Rotorua in the midsection of the North Island of New Zealand

photo courtesy of Small World Productions

The Hidden Valley of Orakei Korako. Dinosaurs walked here sixty-five million years ago, and the impression is that not much has changed, though in fact much has, most of it in the last blink of time.

photo courtesy of Small World Productions

Between the tendrils of steam and mist is the cauldron celebrated as the Wairakei Terraces, in the heart of a valley called Waiora, which means "healthy water."

photo courtesy of Didrik Johnck

Inside the cave of the Kaikoura Winery

photo courtesy of Didrik Johnck

The takahē. It walks like a chicken on big webbed feet but has the oversize, arched red beak of a dodo. It was thought to be extinct until 1948. Now, nineteen of these flightless fowl are on the island, and about two hundred seventy are left in the world.

Ian Murray, Marlborough Man

photo courtesy of Sarah Givens

Using pedal power to reach the natural power of the Brooklyn Wind Turbine

photo courtesy of Small World Productions

Māori believe that all things—rivers, trees, mountains, and the mist—have a life force, and that we are all inextricably bound together by a genealogical web and share in the unfolding frond of the universe.

Crew: Karel Bauer, Patty Conroy, Richard Bangs, and Laura Hubber

photo courtesy of Sarah Givens

How does a capital city with a political administration promoting environmental responsibility and leadership set an example? I ask Ian as we head over to a shop called Mud Cycles to rent some spoked steeds.

The answer is blowin' in the wind, he says with a groan, and he offers to show me.

New Zealand has met the growth in its energy demand over the past thirty years mainly through nonrenewable resources, just like the rest of the world. In 2004, only about one-third of the country's primary energy supply came from renewable sources. Another third came from imported oil, with the remainder from local natural gas and local and imported coal.

But New Zealand is a drafty place—Wellington especially, sitting as it does in the "Roaring Forties" latitudes—and so wind could be a mighty source of power. Chicago would be breathless here. In 1968, a ferryboat, the *Wahine,* whooshed off course onto Barrett Reef and sank with a loss of fifty-two lives. It was one of the country's worst tragedies. The culprit: the wind, roaring at about 138 miles per hour.

Brooklyn is a leafy suburb of Wellington, brightly colored with weatherboard houses on steep hillsides. Inexplicably, most of the main streets are named after U.S. presidents. We head out with bike guide Ricky Pincott, pushing up a steep incline, up a crooked road, up Brooklyn Hill. On the way up, Wellington Harbor is veiled behind a screen of clouds that sometimes thickens, sometimes parts, sometimes drifts over the city. Ricky evidences no trouble with the rigors of the ascent. I click to the end of my gears and pedal as hard I can, my heart pounding. We veer off for a bit onto something called the Car Parts Trail, so named because it runs just beneath the precipitous road, and its bosky edges are decorated with fenders, tires, and other detritus from various wrong turns over the years. At some points, a bushy tree with large, soft leaves grows over the trail. Ian calls it *rangiora,* or "bush-man's toilet paper."

Tuataras are reptiles, but also very different from lizards, crocodiles and amphibians. Their primitive body structure suggests that they have changed little in the past 220 million years, making them among the world's oldest and most unevolved species. In Māori, tuatara means "spiny back."

The single track winds around the western perimeter of the predator-proof fence of the Karori Wildlife Sanctuary, the world's first urban, pest-free conservation wilderness. It's a haven for endangered native birds and wildlife such as the little spotted kiwi, the saddleback, and the tuatara, the lizardlike creature that is the closest living relative to the dinosaur.

The track, though, is narrow, rocky, and too steep for my aptitude, so we veer back onto the road. But even pavement is not all that much better. It is impossible to make a straight line, so I zigzag back and forth, tacking the bike upward. Several times I pivot and cycle across the road perpendicular to my route and then turn, like a good environmentalist, to recycle the same ground.

At more than one bend, I think of just quitting and walking to the top. But this is New Zealand, the estate of unbending will when it comes to adventure sports, so I continue to test my mettle with the pedal. My lungs burn. I try to think other thoughts as I grunt around yet another curve, try to send my mind to a better place, but I can't think of one. I try to imagine the sound of one hand clapping, of one foot pedaling. The sweat from my brow streams into my eyes, blurring my vision, and the summit seems to roll back with every bend as though on wheels. As we climb higher, the light has a strange, oblique intensity that gives Ricky a tranced look and imbues the landscapes with the appearance of being immobilized under a sheen of clear ice.

Presently, I yaw to a level touchstone and become part of the sky. The wind blows hard here, and I plant my feet squarely and grip my handlebars to keep from tipping. Under the whine of the wind, though, is another sound, like a clothes dryer midcycle, a kind of tonal pulsing. Looking down through the clouds, I see scattered and scudding pieces of the harbor in search of a mosaic. The sun hovers, glowing and hot, like the tip of a lit cigar. This could be the viewpoint of the gods.

But then I turn around and look up what appears to be a long, white spear with a periwinkle on top, a spinning vantage that stands above all else. This is the Brooklyn Wind Turbine.

The turbine was built in 1993 as part of a research project, now stands as the oldest such device in New Zealand, and is considered one of the best-performing of its class in the world. It possesses perhaps the best view in the city and the entire south coast, with an unobstructed exposure to the prevailing winds. Its nacelle is 101 feet above the ground, and each of its three blades is almost 45 feet long. It powers the equivalent of about eighty homes a year (it feeds the main electrical grid). It has run at full potential for almost 48 percent of the time, with a peak of 55 percent in 1994, a world record. The international average is just 23 percent.

Wind turbines now produce just 2 percent of New Zealand's

power—about one hundred seventy megawatts, enough for about seventy-six thousand homes—but that figure could reach 20 percent or even more, the Wind Energy Association says, if the government doesn't blow it. Such possibilities do raise the question: why is there only one in Wellington, a city with some of the most consistent winds in the world? As testament to the unreserved might of the *ha,* the breath of spirits, there are municipal and private wind sculptures at every turn.

In some ways, the growing movement to renewable energy reflects the growing power of Māori in government. For most of New Zealand's existence, Māori were marginalized and not recognized in the halls of parliament or officialdom. But of late, several have found a voice, and persuasion. I went to visit one such voice in official offices in Wellington, Andrew Luke, the indigenous conservation ethic manager at the Department of Conservation. Originally, the DOC, created in the late nineteenth century, was a mechanism of land grab for the Crown, preserving places for the aesthetic and recreational enjoyment of European immigrants. But now, if there is a government arm that comes close to promoting and practicing the tenets of kaitiakitanga, it is the DOC. Andrew, who has been at the department for less than three years, has witnessed some of the changes. He gives me an example: the evolving policies regarding the wood pigeon. Only recently, the DOC has taken a hard-line, Calvinistic view of preservation and protection, meaning that if an animal was deemed in some way threatened, then there could be no sanctioned taking of such. But Māori, including Hēmi, who served for years in the DOC, have slowly helped recraft the thinking toward a policy of wise sustainability. Māori have always hunted wood pigeons for food as well as feathers for traditional cloaks, but have taken the birds in numbers that assured a healthy population. They never hunted for sport or to excess, Andrew says. Now, after much debate, the wood pigeon is fair game for Māori, who also have access to certain plants, animals, fish, and drupes for medicinal and other traditional purposes. It's all part of a mind-set shift that has migrated into energy and other arenas.

Meridian Energy is the state-owned company that runs the Brooklyn Wind Turbine, a model renewable-energy generator that doesn't directly produce carbon dioxide emissions.

However, like any company, Meridian does produce a carbon footprint with its day-to-day operations, such as land and air travel. But Meridian, like many concerns in New Zealand and, increasingly, around the world, offsets any contributions to greenhouse gases by purchasing enough carbon credits to balance out the emissions. It also offers carbon credits to families and small businesses.

Now Meridian is planning a project called West Wind, a seventy-turbine wind farm west of Wellington. It will be the largest in the Southern Hemisphere, which will further move the city and the state toward the goal of carbon neutrality.

Wander along the promenade around the edge of beautiful Wellington Harbour, just meters from the bustling city streets. Take time out to discover sculptures, bars, and eateries along the way. You can relax on the sand at Oriental Bay or hike up to find panoramic views at the top of Mount Victoria.

POWER LUNCH

Na tāu rourou, na tāku rourou, ka ora ai te iwi.

With your food basket and my food basket, people will be nourished.

After all this power biking, the impulse for a power lunch is not resisted, so we head downtown to Logan Brown.

The restaurant is based in a colonnaded 1920s banking chamber on the corner of Cuba and Vivian streets. Despite its august milieu, it has a reputation for running a kaitiakitanga kitchen.

I meet Alister Brown, the convivial, saturnalian coowner and chief chef, and he invites me to join him in preparing his signature lunch, blackfoot paua ravioli. (*Paua* is the Māori name for New Zealand's endemic abalone.)

I live in California, where abalone was once considered an abundant resource but has declined to alarmingly low levels. Commercial abalone fishing is illegal, as is the purchase of wild abalone. As a result, few restaurants feature abalone.

But here it is a signature dish. Alister puts me to work stamping out circles from pancakes of thin buckwheat pasta, within which he rolls dollops of paua. He will then serve a plate of four to the luncheon, at NZ$30. He holds up the shell of today's paua. It is gray with encrustations on the outside, but as he turns it over, there is a burst of iridescence: intense, swirling greens, blues, purples, and pinks. It is one of the world's most attractive shells.

I ask Alister how his restaurant can offer a resource that is in danger of disappearing throughout much of the world. His answer is simply that the resource is doing well here in New Zealand, thank you, because of wise management and smart servicing, as in his kitchen. "Paua is a delicacy, like truffles, and we mince it and serve it up in very small portions so a diner can appreciate the taste like a gourmand rather than a glutton."

Alister also describes some of the astute policies New Zealand imposes to ensure the sustainability of paua. Though it is gathered recreationally and commercially, strict catch limits are set for both ways of harvesting. For recreational fishers, the limit is ten paua of each species (blackfoot and yellowfoot) per person per day, and they can be caught only by free diving (no scuba gear). And it is forbidden to take young paua. The minimum legal size for the blackfoot paua Alister is serving today is 125 millimeters, which indicates an age of about fifteen. Alister says the large, oval shell he holds up for today's lunch crowd is about sixty years old.

It all sounds similar to John Panoho's third pointer: "Notice that when a Māori takes shellfish from the sea, he takes enough for his family, but no more."

To Māori, paua are taonga, esteemed both as an important source of *kai* (food) and as a valued resource for traditional arts and crafts. Paua are often used to represent the eyes in Māori carvings and are associated with the stars, or *whetu*, the eyes of ancestors that gaze down from the night sky.

But when I ask Alister why New Zealand has such good thinking when it comes to paua and other limited resources, he has a different theory.

"It's the OE."

The OE is the Overseas Experience, something that has evolved into an active part of the Kiwi culture. Because the country is at the bottom of the planet, isolated and compact, not burdened by too much history, it has put great value on foreign travel. When the First World War broke out in 1914, a higher proportion of New Zealanders went overseas than did residents of any other country. And today, because it is a non-saber-rattling member of the world community, its citizens are welcome to travel almost every place, and they do. Most will shoulder a backpack and take off between college and profession, and as citizens of the Commonwealth, they can easily find short-term employment in other member countries. While, by most reckonings, less than 20 percent of American adults even possess a passport, more than 78 percent of Kiwis do. What does that mean?

Well, according to Alister, the OE allows a heightened awareness of the rest of the world, an ability to witness, often firsthand, what is working and what is not on the global stage and to behold the interconnectedness of all things. It allows New Zealanders a visionary perspective—to be able to skate to where the puck is going, not to where it's been.

Amid the insular reckonings of much of the world, posited by people who often have barely ventured beyond their own borders, New Zealanders, by the time they are in positions of political or economic power, have had the chance to observe a raft of faraway initiatives and their consequences. That experience includes the surveying of sustainability policies in all walks, including those governing the harvesting of food from the sea.

A towering appetite all this promotes, and so finally we retire to the stately dining room for a "paua lunch." It is a simple presentation— a light butter-and-lemon sauce, a hint of garlic, mixed for texture with kumara, the sweet potato brought to Aotearoa by the first Māori navigators. The plump, round ravioli tastes like the food of the gods. "We don't like to have jingles and bells on the plate," Alister explains. "We don't like to have architectural food. It's about sourcing good product, gathering it as fresh as can be, treating it with respect, and cooking it simply."

The respect part of the equation seems a relatively new factor for Alister and many other Pakeha. Alister grew up in Wairarapa, about two hours from Wellington, on a sheep and cattle ranch and developed a passion for hunting and fishing early. "When I was a child out fishing, I took all I wanted. It was like a competition: the more you took, the better the sportsman you were. It was all for the photo. Take as many as you can, eat a couple, and leave the rest to rot."

For Alister's OE, he first went to the United States, where he picked up his culinary arts degree at the New England Culinary Institute. He then worked in several restaurants around the world and saw how resource mismanagement and lack of respect for the environments that supplied dinner tables were affecting the quality and quantity of foods. Along with many other Kiwis of his generation, he had an awakening and returned home to endorse the thinking that Māori had been promoting for centuries. "Now we only take what we need, and maybe a little for our neighbor. We now look after the resource for our children and theirs."

It is not, I conclude between ambrosial bites, so much an enlightened approach, but rather the paua of positive thinking.

To work off lunch, I decide to paddle out into the great blue bowl that is Wellington Harbor, renting a banana-colored boat from Fergs Kayaks on Queens Wharf.

The protected harbor has a sinuous, mouthlike shape, evoking the legend of Maui and his prodigious catch. As the story goes, when the fish was hauled up, its mouth formed a lake separated from the sea by a barrier of land. The lake trapped a sea monster named Ngake, who didn't like being trapped, so he broke through to the open sea, creating today's harbor entrance.

Little there is as satisfying as messing about in a kayak. Though I am surrounded by the hum of a great city in action, the paddle is a quiet and contemplative glide, almost a sort of meditation. The air is as dank as an abalone. The wind seems asleep. I can feel my arms connected to the water. The low afternoon sun doesn't just gleam on the Victorian houses above the bay. The glow is deeper than that. The red and orange that light up the facades seem to come from within. It's as if the light contains some special MSG of sight, turning the city luminous and dreamlike.

There is nothing quite as perfect as a kayak. Perfection is attained not when there is no longer anything to add, such as in a rich man's yacht, but when there is no longer anything to take away, such as with a craft like this, stripped down to its nakedness.

Paddling solo, making long cracks on the surface sheen, I feel a raw, immediate happiness, the clean freedom of a hobo. But my mind drifts to the imponderable origins of kaitiakitanga. The original "Vikings of the sea" paddled these same beryl waters, moving from island to island throughout the Pacific, thinking perhaps that food and land were without limit. Many motes, such as Easter Island, they devastated with overuse before moving on to the next. Aotearoa was the world's last major landmass to be colonized, and it must have been a shock to discover that beyond it was nothing but negative space and ice. The voyagers had come to the end of the biddable earth. It may have been that as the original explorers went back to the islands where they had left the environment in ruins, there was a slow realization that resources were not limitless and that if there were to be a future, the culture had to organize around the idea of guardianship.

My paddle swallows yards with each stroke, but then the ferry from Picton comes charging into the harbor, sending out huge waves in its wake. My boat begins to crankle as though drunk, and I know it's time to head back to solid ground.

That evening, as a complement to the elegant and delicate lunch, I head over to Majoribanks Street. I visit the Māori-owned and -operated eatery called Kai in the City for a postmodern version of a *hāngi,* a meal traditionally cooked in the earth with hot rocks and steam—a progenitor to the Slow Food movement. Bill Hamilton, a local Māori politician, is the conductor for the experience, saying, "We don't sell food; we sell *manaaki*," the Māori term for hospitality. "And we tell our stories." None-theless, in the crammed, six-table room, we sample a huge array of what might be called fusion Māori foods, such as mutton bird pâté, flaxseed bread, kūmara mash, smoked eel, horopito berries, karengo (seaweed) fronds, sea eggs, sea urchins—there is no suffering from malacia here—all washed down with Tohu Pinot Noir. And then Bill Hamilton hands out sheets of lyrics, shakes his gray mane, lifts his guitar, and tells us we have to sing for our supper: it is not optional. We all join in, with our best karaoke voices, belting the Māori love song, "Pōkarekare Ana":

Pōkarekare ana	They are agitated,
Ngā wai o Waiapu,	The waters of Waiapu,
Whiti atu koe hine	But when you cross over, girl
Marino ana e.	They will be calm.
E hine e	Oh, girl,
Hoki mai ra.	Return to me,
Ka mate ahau	I could die
I te aroha e.	Of love for you.
Tuhituhi taku reta	I have written my letter,
Tuku atu taku rīngi,	I have sent my ring,
Kia kite tō iwi	So that your people can see
Raru raru ana e.	That I am troubled.
Whati whati taku pene	My pen is shattered,
Ka pau aku pepa,	I have no more paper,
Ko taku aroha	But my love
Mau tonu ana e.	Is still steadfast.
E kore te aroha	My love will never
E maroke i te rā,	Be dried by the sun,
Mākūkū tonu i	It will be forever moistened
Aku roimata e.	By my tears.

146

Sated in all the senses, I head back to the hotel to bed. It is a restless night, and I am not sure if it is the piri piri pepper dressing, the kūmara pie I shoveled down, or my subconscious wandering through the many rooms of kaitiakitanga. I think I hear the voice of a morepork, the owl that Māori believe is an ancestral guardian spirit. It makes a sound like a dark brushstroke on the night, but we're in the city, so I can't be sure. I wonder if I have seen enough and should head home.

Paua shells are often used to represent the eyes in Māori carvings and are associated with the stars, or whetu, *the eyes of ancestors that gaze down from the night sky.*

ONE TOUCH OF NATURE MAKES THE WHOLE WORLD KIN

E mōhiotia ana a waho kei roto he aha.

One cannot know from the outside what is contained within.

S ometimes less sleep means you are more awake. With the morning, I decide I have not yet seen my fill, so I head over to another enterprise that is stewarding in a far-reaching way.

It is an operation called Global Volunteer Network, which locally has been gifted by Māori with the name "Ngā Kaitiaki," as the volunteers are "the guardians" of a plot of threatened forest within the city limits.

The program invites people from around the world who want to make a difference to come here and undertake lucubrations to preserve, monitor, and reestablish the natural environment. It began about five years ago with volunteers from the neighborhood. Then volunteers started coming from around the Wellington region. And then about four years ago it became an international proposition.

I meet Dr. Dan Rollinson, the resident ecologist, who promptly leads me beneath a wooden gable board decorated with a carved Māori mask flashing iridescent paua-shell eyes and extending a scary-looking tongue. It is a traditional *koruru* mask, representing an ancestral chief, and is meant to keep guard over the *marae,* a sacred place for intertribal religious and social ceremonies; the name literally means "the place cleared, free of weeds." The protruding tongue signifies defiance toward an enemy and certainly gives a visitor pause.

We cross a wooden bridge and snake down a goat track into a small river canyon, eventually reaching the Otari-Wilton's Bush revegetation project. Wellington is a city of trees, but almost all today are introduced species. Otari-Wilton's Bush is the largest tract of original native forest in central Wellington, with more than a thousand plants growing in a five-hectare area.

Job Wilton, a farsighted local farmer, in 1860 set aside a small patch of forest to be protected from stock. Other swaths in the area were cleared for farming and development and never replenished.

Rubbish and invasive weeds have devastated a section along the Kaiwharawhara Stream, the main Wellington freshwater flow. The hope is that newly planted native trees will help reinstate the original habitat, bringing back not only native birds but also fish. The area was once densely shaded, and native fish finned through water that did not vary greatly in temperature. As the trees were cleared, the sun shone directly on the water, the temperature began to vary, the ecosystem changed, and the fish died. So, to restore the life in the stream, the vegetation beside the stream needs to be restored.

*A traditional **koruru** mask, representing an ancestral chief, is meant to keep guard over the **marae**, a sacred place for intertribal religious and social ceremonies. The name literally means "the place cleared, free of weeds."*

Garden-gloved men and women from all over the world are with Dan. Under his watchful eye, and my curious one, they set about rewilding this patch, pulling weeds and blackberry bushes and measuring planted endemics (brought here in milk cartons), such as the makomako (New Zealand wineberry); the bushy lemonwood tree; the whauwhaupaku, or five finger tree; and the kohoho, or poroporo, whose leaves and unripe fruit are deadly. They now all grow in thick profusion, as the original Māori might have found them.

One volunteer, twenty-eight-year-old Maureen McQueen, from Limerick City, Ireland, takes a break from clearing gorse and describes her decision to take her holiday covered in dirt. "It's just a different way of seeing New Zealand. When you're a tourist, you miss out on the country sometimes because you're just going to the tourist spots. So I suppose this is one way of experiencing New Zealand's wilds, and yeah, you really get into it big time. You're out there in the environment, and yeah, it's nice to make a contribution and meet up with a bunch of like-minded people and to just do something physical, you know, instead of just traveling around, aimlessly. It's good to have a purpose, you know?"

Jonathan Kennett, a local ecologist, a mountain-bike guide author, and the project coordinator for the revegetation effort, explains that volunteers typically spend just one or two days a month working on a specific site, then move on to another project: seal surveying, dolphin monitoring, silviculturing, dune restoring, trail building, or predator controlling. I wonder if that little amount of time can actually make a difference.

"It's interesting, isn't it?" Jonathan says. "I think a lot of people don't actually do anything to support the environment or their community because they think they're just one individual, and what difference can one possibly make? But it reminds me of a saying that my father told me a long time ago: 'No man made a greater mistake than he who did nothing because he could do only a little.' "

The birdsong here is like a small spring singing to itself among the stones. The place seems intimate, the world writ small. I ask Dan why an organization with such global reach is based here in New Zealand—why not Geneva or New York or some more-considered epicenter?—and he echoes the OE theory. "New Zealanders love to travel, and perhaps because of the natural assets here, they love to travel to wilderness regions. They see how wild landscapes in other parts of the world have been devastated and recognize how unique the flora and fauna here are, and when they return, they take a heightened interest in preservation. Global Volunteers was spawned from that consciousness." It is true that New Zealand has been so long separate from other land that it is sometimes regarded as forming a distinct botanical region; as much as three-quarters of its flora is distinctive and specific to this strange and wonderful antediluvian life raft.

And Dan believes that lessons learned and applied here, often by visiting overseas volunteers, need to be carried back and spread to all corners. "Everybody really needs to take stock of what natural assets they have in their own backyard and do their bit to preserve what they have. It's something that should be spread around the world."

Wellington may not be a harmonic convergence point on the world map, but it is certainly a paua point. Before heading out of town, I stop into Kura Contemporary Ethnic Art, one of the many galleries on Allen Street in downtown Wellington. It is overflowing with paua masks, necklaces, bracelets, amulets, jewelry of every sort, even bowls of paua shells to finger and admire. It's easy to see why Māori regard the shell with such reverence, as it almost seems a magic ingress to a spirit world, an eye to beyond the void. Holding one large, swirling piece, I almost believe I can glimpse the meaning of kaitiakitanga.

The cup of Wellington's fortunes has emptied and filled like that of the whole of the country, and of late it is brimming: it seems a city of hope, a metropolis of moxie, celebrating its cultural traditions while mapping a clear path to the future. One of the icons of this newfound sense of promise is the Te Papa Tongarewa (Our Repository of Treasures), the contrapuntal national museum, opened in 1998 at a cost of NZ$140 million, free to the public, poised like a floating beacon on the edge of the harbor.

As I approach from the City to Sea Bridge, it appears from the outside a billowing smattering of airfoil architectural styles—bold curves, blocks, and glass—that seem in favor for contemporary public buildings in much of the world. It looks designed by committee and could be another result of the storied OE. Perhaps traveling New Zealanders have been exposed to so many designs that work in certain settings that they brought them together here as the national attic. Whether it works or not is the subject of much debate within the country, with the building passionately deconstructed and appraised by Māori and Pakeha alike. I am gently drawn into the sweeping entrance, meant to be a *waharoa*, a gateway, but once inside I am swept away by its five floors of taonga, art, artifacts, weapons, and stories. Around everything is an epidermis of narrative by which the world is rendered intelligible. I am sucked into this rabbit hole and spend hours immersed in the etiological and bicultural quiddity that gives Aotearoa its shape and spirit. I am in awe of a thirty-man, nineteenth-century war canoe, a fifteenth-century great house, and the bone fishhooks, woven garments, feathered cloaks, stone tools, genealogical sticks, and delicately carved sacred greenstones pulled from the rivers of the South Island. Everyone on this land was once an immigrant, and the museum seems to have been imagined as a cultural diversity bridge. Its centerpiece is its updated single-gable marae, adorned with carvings of a Chinese dragon, a Samoan tapa, an English rose, an Irish shamrock, and a Southern European acanthus leaf, all meant to symbolize the people sharing this land.

Sharing it, however, has not been easy. Māori are still scarred by the 1840 Treaty of Waitangi, which led to Britain's annexation of New Zealand and the expropriation of Māori lands. Although some Māori chiefs originally welcomed the treaty as a way to stem the flow of settlers and guns, things did not work out that way. Te Papa's interactive exhibit about the treaty boldly examines these raw scars. In exchange for granting sovereignty to Queen Victoria, Māori were promised the rights of British subjects and undisturbed possession of their lands.

In the early nineteenth century, as European immigrants flooded in and took away Māori land, many Māori were driven to desperation and wars. The Crown continued to confiscate Māori lands, and by the 1880s, the Māori population—which numbered about two hundred thousand in 1840—was less than forty thousand, having been wiped out by wars and imported pathogens. Today, because of increased disease resistance, intermarriage and a high birth rate, the number of people who identify themselves as Māori in the national census has swelled to more than five hundred thousand—about 15 percent of the New Zealand population. And in 1975, the Treaty of Waitangi was reconsidered, and the Waitangi Tribunal was set up to try to correct the land-rights abuses of the previous century.

The centerpiece in Te Papa is its single-gable marae, an updated version of the traditional sacred meeting ground adorned with carvings of a Chinese dragon, a Samoan tapa, an English rose, an Irish shamrock, and a Southern European acanthus leaf, all meant to symbolize the people sharing this land.

MOA'S ARK

Kia kōrero koe i te ngutu o te manu,
Kia hoki ana mai tō wairua ki te ao nei!

Speak with the bill of a bird,
Let your soul come back to us in this world!

After we have kicked around Wellington for a few days, it's time to again head north, the way a white heron might. We traverse the western coast for a few miles to a beach called Paraparaumu, across from what could be Skull Island. A small metal catamaran, the MV *Te Aihe,* awaits on the beach, but before we can board, we have to undergo an exercise new to my repertoire: a rat check. Under the eagle eye of Māori Tourism Council chief John Barrett, we open all our bags and rifle through all the contents to prove no rats are about to stow away on our little trip.

A big bird of an orange and yellow tractor on monster wheels tows us into the surf; the two Honda outboards are fired up, and we skid across Waiorua Bay toward a cobbled beach at the northern end of the island. In these same waters, John Barrett lost two daughters, ages eight and six, in 1986 when a catamaran they were in sank as they were dragging in nets.

John rolls down an aluminum gangplank, and we step into the euphonious opera that is Kapiti Island.

A short tread over the foam-furled rocks and past a line of driftwood, and we are in a wide ecotone busy with birds—a Moa's Ark of birds. There are weka, kakariki, New Zealand pigeons, moreporks, whiteheads, North Island robins, North Island tomtits, fantails, and the famous bellbirds of Māori song and fable. We're in a twitchers' paradise; we're in birdland!

The weka, famously fearless and cheeky, has no compunction about stealing my PowerBar with its hooked beak when I turn my head to another bird sound. In contrast, the kakariki, a red-crowned parakeet, is a rather shy bird, and we can't even get close enough for a good photo.

There, there is the takahē. It walks like a chicken on big, webbed feet, but has the oversize, arched red beak of a dodo. It was thought to be extinct until 1948. Now, nineteen of these flightless fowl are on the island, and about two hundred seventy are left in the world.

And the metallic-green plumage means the fat and happy kereu (New Zealand pigeon) is rustling around in the grass and clover, puffing its white tuxedo chest like a robber baron.

As I circle about this aviary, something alights on my shoulder. My instinct is to duck and brush it away, but it has a firm grip on my sweater, and a glance at its powerful, curved bill and its quizzically cocked face gives me pause. It is a kaka, or bush parrot, a relative of the infamous kea, and it practically gives me a hongi. From a distance the kaka looks a drab brown, but on my shoulder I can see in its tiled feathers subtle combinations of bronzy greens and browns tinged with shiny red and maroon below the wings. Māori fable says the kaka tricked his cousin, the prettier, brighter-colored kakariki, by telling him he would catch more insects and thrive if he were not so bright. So the kakariki gave the kaka his brilliant red feathers. The kaka, too, was threatened for a time, not just because of its plumage, but also because of its taste. In 1849 one colonialist wrote home that "the large parrots make the most delicious soup."

Whiteheads (bush canaries) are the most common birds on Kapiti. They flit about the forest like gaudy bits of paper, searching the trees and shrubs for insects.

The islands of Aotearoa were predator-free for most of their existence, until the arrival of man and his pests, especially rats. Without any need to worry about carnivorous quadrupeds, many birds shed their ability to fly and now possess only trifling leftovers of wings. The first snake to enter this terrestrial paradise was man, a millennium ago. Over time, human invaders brought rats, dogs, cats, stoats, goats, opossums, and other foreign species. Many ground birds couldn't outrun the new mammalian predators and fell to the vanishing point, more than fifty on this island alone.

Recognizing that New Zealand birds were flying into the glass of extinction, a group lobbied for declaring Kapiti Island a public reserve and succeeded in 1897. But there was little weight behind the designation, and it stopped few hunters and collectors. Over the years, Kapiti has withstood the onslaughts of 1840s whalers, aerial chemical pest-control sprays, bushfires, goat and pig farming, rat colonies, and brush-tailed opossum infestation.

In 1949, access to the island was restricted (only fifty visitors a day are allowed). Finally, in 1977, the government designated Kapiti Island a full-fledged reserve, though the north end was allowed to be safeguarded by the descendants of the original Māori owners, who together run a nature lodge and an ecotourism operation called Kapiti Island Alive.

As a part of managing the island, various bold programs to recover its early balance were undertaken. From 1980 to 1986, some twenty-two thousand five hundred opossums were killed, and nary a one has been sighted since. In 1996, a similar program to poison kiore (Polynesian rats) and Norway rats was undertaken. Sustained by the visitor bag checks, it too is deemed successful. Three thousand rat bait stations now ring the coastline of Kapiti Island—the first line of defense against rats that might arrive on floating debris or passing boats.

The island's own immunological response, and the tonic of time, have given new health and hope to the birdlife. Some utopists have even suggested that DNA samplings of the moa, the man-sized bird that early Māori hunted to extinction, could be used to bioengineer a new generation, and that Kapiti could be an ideal Jurassic Park.

The cobbled beach of Kapiti Island

Māori lore says that Kapiti is a divine Stargate where a warrior finds spiritual healing. Now it is a place for the healing of native plant and birdlife, which I imagine in Māori cosmology is a distinction without a difference.

We step up to the modest common house and are met by a multigenerational line of oil-dark eyes—Māori family members who sing a welcome song with guitar accompaniment and then one by one greet us with a gentle pressing of the nose and forehead.

We settle into the small eco-lodge, a former kids' camp, now a spruced-up bunkhouse in a field of flax, with takahē running around like sheep. After dropping off our bags and checking the room flashlights, we return for a smorgasbord of freshly baked bread, crayfish, and mussels, all consumed along with tales from paterfamilias John Barrett. John has the blunt pate, the wire-rim glasses and the soft, antiphonal voice of a South Pacific Gandhi. When I ask him his title within the family organization

The small metal catamaran, the MV Te Aihe, awaits on the beach, but before guests can board, they have to undergo an unusual exercise: a rat check.

he says, "Lucky Person." He says he is lucky to be here, lucky to be a descendant of a grandmother who took steps to allow his family a home on this treasured island. "Our operation is really just a continuation of what my grandma started in the early 1900s. It's an old Māori practice of *manaakitanga,* which is an obligation to provide hospitality for visitors."

No other place in New Zealand has such a density and diversity of birdlife, because of the century-long effort to rid the island of predators. "Last summer, for the first time in forty years, I saw flocks of two hundred wood pigeons and similar-sized flocks of juvenile tui and bellbirds," John says.

160

The birdsong volume has gradually been dialed up in Kapiti. Last spring was the best and loudest John has ever heard—exceptionally cacophonous because of a combination of weather patterns, rising bird populations, and unusually abundant food sources, which began increasing in 2005. On the mainland, however, these songs are hushed. Some of New Zealand's most iconic locations, such as the Milford Track, look wildly beautiful, but they remain relatively devoid of the sounds of birds. Not Kapiti, which at times seems to screech with delight.

"If we're able to continue this way, I am sure in fifty years' time it will allow visitors a glimpse of what Aotearoa might have looked like prior to humans arriving here," John says. "It won't look exactly the same, because we've lost fifty species, but give it a hundred years and we'll get as close as possible."

John is a big believer not just in avifauna preservation but also in Māori cultural preservation, and he considers that the latter can be achieved through storytelling. "There's an old Māori saying that you have to look back to go forward," he says.

"If we don't tell our stories, others will," he warns. "Don't let others commoditize our culture."

In the late 1940s, Sir Peter Buck, a prominent Māori leader and onetime member of Parliament, lamented the passing of traditions. The notorious war dance, the haka, graphically tells the story of a Māori chief, Te Rauparaha, who while fleeing his enemies went through an Elisabeth Kübler-Ross range of emotions. It is a story told through brazen movements and furious sounds, meant for Māori eyes and ears, but it was dressed up and turned into a show for visiting dignitaries. That evolved into an eye-bulging burlesque for tourists and the opening dance number for New Zealand's premier rugby team, the All Blacks. There's more culture in a cup of yogurt than in most of today's haka shows.

A 1913 survey showed that 90 percent of Māori schoolkids could speak their ancestral language, even though early Pakeha authorities prohibited Te Reo Māori from being spoken in schools. For decades, Māori stayed away from their own heritage in droves. They felt ashamed; they wanted to be Pakeha. They refused their own words, ignored their own stories. Another survey in 1995 revealed that only 7 percent of Māori youth were fluent in their ancestors' tongue. (John Panoho told me that if he spoke Te Reo Māori in school when he was a child, his knuckles were rapped.) The survey also suggested that the language and all its concepts, such as kaitiakitanga, were in danger of extinction because most fluent speakers were older than forty-five, and mortality rates were high. It was a pale, tabescent period for the culture.

Now, though, a renaissance is under way as Māori focus on self-determination and on regaining their tribal lands, language, art and culture, and identity. Some trace the beginnings of this resurgence to the 1970s, when the Black Power movement in the United States inspired indigenous peoples around the world. But it is burning brightly today, led by artists, storytellers, and entrepreneurs. The singer Hinewehi Mohi, who sings only in Te Reo Māori, recently said, "People ask me to translate the lyrics, and I shrug and say, 'Why?'"

Today, about a quarter of the Māori population speaks the native language, and nearly half are younger than twenty-five. There are twenty-one tribal radio stations and a Māori television network. And there is an increasing community of proud storytellers.

And so John Barrett tells stories of men who transformed into birds at will and accounts of his ancestors' bloody battles. While under attack from an opposing tribe, the fearsome warrior Te Rauparaha swam three miles to the mainland for help, bringing so many canoes to the bay that "sunlight couldn't touch water." Nonetheless, he lost the fight, and legend claims that his body is buried in one of the coastal caves and that his restless spirit haunts the island today.

After dark, John offers to take us for a night walk in search of New Zealand's avian eminence, the charismatic national symbol, the elusive kiwi. "I'd say 99.9 percent of New Zealanders haven't seen a kiwi," John supposes. "And Kapiti is probably the most reliable place in the country to find them."

Before the arrival of Pakeha in Aotearoa, the little ratite relative to the moa was highly prized by Māori as food and a source of feathers for ceremonial cloaks. But soon after the nocturnal bird's "discovery" by Europeans in the early 1800s, the kiwi became popular for its odd attributes. Its nostrils are near the tip of its prodigious Pinocchio beak instead of at the base as with other birds. It has no tail, and its wings are vestigial, nearly invisible. Its feathers, more like fur, don't sport the barbules possessed by other birds, and it lays an egg of gigantic proportions for its body size: about 20 percent of its body weight.

The female is substantially larger than the male, and it alone incubates the eggs to produce miniature replicas of its parents, complete with feathers, unlike the downy fledglings of other birds.

Once known in Europe, the kiwi became sought-after to be added to museum and private collections and to make fashionable muffs worn by upper-class Victorian women.

163

There are records from 1885 of one collector killing more than two thousand two hundred kiwis for the European market. By the time the birds were protected by law in 1896, kiwi numbers had dwindled so drastically that the bird was considered very rare. Today perhaps seventy-five thousand kiwi birds are left in the wild, and numbers are declining. Stoats (relatives of weasels and ferrets), brought here in the 1880s to try to control rabbits (also nonnative), kill about 70 percent of kiwi chicks before the birds reach six months old. The prospectus is far from positive, until islands of hope such as Kapiti are factored in.

The little spotted kiwi has long been absent from the North Island mainland and now survives in North Island environs only on Kapiti Island, where about one thousand one hundred are in residence, the largest population in the world.

About fifteen of us, Māori and Pakeha, head out in single file along one of the labyrinthine paths, hoping to spot one of the little spotted kiwis out digging for bush worms and grubs. The island seems immensely expanded by darkness, the breathing, living, tarry darkness of Kapiti after the sun. We lean into the night, stepping over gnarled roots that look like the toes of some ancient bird. John, in the lead, whispers back to us in a thin, raspy voice, like a debarked dog: "I'll have the torch in front of me, so you need to be close together, bunched up tight. Quiet is important, and if you hear a noise that I've missed, let me know."

After crunching along the trail for several minutes, we see what looks like a little ghost pad into the grass.

"Follow me quickly. They go really quickly. See that? Oh yeah. That was definitely the big bum of a kiwi. I could tell by the sound: *prerh.*"

Then two more bolt through the light and rustle away on stumpy legs. A bird in the bush is worth two in the hand. Another makes a rasorial race down the path, tapping its long bill side to side. And then one magically waddles by my boot, looking very much like a penguin. It is a penguin! A little blue penguin, the world's smallest, a dapper lad who gives me a glance from his yellow eyes and then sets his short legs scurrying, round body swaying, making a snorelike call, finally disappearing into the night.

The national bird of New Zealand, the elusive nocturnal kiwi. Today perhaps seventy-five thousand kiwi birds are left in the wild, and numbers are declining.

JUST THE FLAX, MA'AM

Ko te rite i aku kamo ki te pua kōrari.
Ka pupuhi te hau, ka maringi te wai e!

My weeping eyes are like the flowers of the flax.
The wind blows, and down comes the nectar!

awake to the sound of liquid notes, the songs of birds in balance, cut a bit by the harsh screech of the koekoea, the migratory long-tailed cuckoo. I wander out into the melody and sit in the grass to watch the sun light the hills. Birds scatter like paint into the sky. For a moment I think they shouldn't be flying loose like this, throwing pigments every which way, as though the skies and trees belong to them, and then I remember that here, they do.

From as far back as legend, Māori have imbued birds with the voices of spirits. In his book *New Zealand: Being a Narrative of Travels and Adventures during a Residence in That Country between the Years 1831 and 1837*, the English trader J. S. Polack describes meeting a chief who at first was greatly afflicted by the death of a son but later seemed quite cheerful. He explained to Polack that as he had been passing a bush, his son, in the form of a little bird, had whistled to him and told him to dry his tears because the son felt perfectly satisfied with the quarters he now occupied. "Shall I grieve at his happiness?" the old man asked. Now, as I walk through this field, there is a blizzard of little birds singing, and several whiteheads career straight into a tangled treetop and out the other side, untouched. I wonder if one might be my friend Tom Peirce letting me know he's well-plumed and happy, unruffled by the passage, doing just fine.

Before heading back to the mainland, I tell John that this island seems a living model of modern conservation, but he shakes his head no. "The word *conservation* is new to us. Conservation does not achieve balance. Conservation is not kaitiakitanga. Let me show you."

John then walks me to a flax bush and recites the same adage that Kylie Ruwhiu-Karawana had sung on the South Island: "if you take out the heart of the flax bush, where will the bellbird sing?" In a voice barely above a whisper, he elaborates. "The flax nourishes our people. We use the fiber for clothing, ropes, baskets, ladders, and cooking; we use the roots as medicine."

Europeans also harvested flax during the maritime heyday of the nineteenth century for the manufacture of ropes, canvas sails, nets, and sacks, without any regard for the interdependencies of the plant. Like timber, seals, and whales, it seemed an inexhaustible resource. Māori knew, though, from hard-won experience that unsustainable use eventually annihilated resources, and so they crafted songs and saws to convey this wisdom.

"The bellbird is attracted to the bright red flowers of the flax," John says. "If the center is pulled from the flax, it won't flower, and the bellbirds won't come, and the story ends."

The olive-green bellbird is a honey eater, with a special tongue like a toothbrush that enables it to sip nectar. When the bellbird pokes its head into a flax flower to reach the nectar, pollen sticks to its head feathers. Then when the bellbird flies to another flower, the pollen brushes onto the sticky stigma, and a seed begins to form, and a new flax plant is born. It is an unbounded game, the endless expression of generosity on behalf of all. As William Blake mused, "If the doors of perception were cleansed everything would appear to man as it is, infinite."

"Kaitiakitanga is a protocol to manage sustainability," John explains while fingering a flax leaf. "It really is saying, 'Please be careful with the resource, as the resource is us, and the future.' Our responsibility as Māori is to ensure that our grandchildren and great-grandchildren can enjoy what we enjoy. It's all about the unborn."

RIVER DANCE

Ko au te awa ko te awa ko au.

I am the river and the river is me.

After returning to the mainland from Kapiti, we continue north around the wide mouth of the South Taranaki Bight to the port town of Wanganui, which means "expansive river mouth" (the town uses the Pakeha spelling, while the river gets the Māori spelling). It was settled by Europeans in 1831 and became for a time the fifth-largest city in New Zealand. Here my twelve-year-old son, Walker, on a school break, catches up with me. He joins us as we head up the Whanganui River Road alongside the country's longest navigable waterway toward the fecund interior. The first European up this passage may have been a trader named Rowe who made a business of brokering preserved Māori heads. On his upriver quest, he met his match and was whacked by a Māori club. His own shriveled, smoke-dried head was then sold to another white trader.

We now make our way to a small aerial cable car that crosses the river to the most unreservedly off-the-grid lodge, The Flying Fox, surrounded by national park, and owned and operated by Annette Main, John Blythe, and Billy the Kid, the resident Jack Russell terrier.

The Flying Fox is less a lodge than an excuse to live a lifestyle. Annette and John have crafted two self-contained cottages from recycled, found, and rescued materials and set them amid their organic gardens and walnut orchards, planted by missionaries a hundred years ago. With their eclectic mishmash of materials and styles, the buildings look like clubhouses built by children for children. The cooking is on woodstoves, the water is heated by solar panels, the toilets are waterless, and the collection of more than a thousand records (featuring favorites Nana Mouskouri, Bob Dylan, Van Morrison, and Bruce Cockburn) is all vinyl.

As we winch across the canyon, the current below makes popping sounds like ice cubes in a drink. As the aerial contraption shudders to a halt, we step to the smell of wet earth and wood smoke. Annette invites us inside the main house, reminiscent of an overgrown house-truck from the hippie era, and serves flat, white coffee and freshly baked organic macadamia biscuits. She tells me she bought the property seventeen years ago, just shy of her fortieth birthday, after her last child had gone to university. Her grandfather was in his nineties. "I thought there was a good chance of having another fifty years of life, looked at what was happening on the planet, and realized there was a good chance New Zealand would become a haven for those whose own countries were becoming spoiled by excesses in consumption and a lack of consideration for the environment."

Annette, I learn, is an elected member and deputy chair representing the Whanganui District on the Regional Council, which has primary responsibility for the guardianship of the water, land, and air of a sizable chunk of the lower North Island. That leads me, of course, to ask my now-habitual question of whether The Flying Fox is an eco-lodge compatible with her understanding of kaitiakitanga.

"We do not regard ourselves as an eco-lodge," she snaps, feeling slighted at being considered in such a category. "Our guest accommodations reflect the choices we make to live more simply, to enjoy our own local food. They reflect our own practice and philosophy of reuse of existing materials and the reduction of waste. If people like the sound of that, then we hope that those who choose to come here enjoy the reminder that it is the simple pleasures, the gift of time and the forgotten values of life, which are important.

"As far as kaitiakitanga, we have put the ownership of our property into a trust, as we believe our role is as guardians of the piece of land we are privileged to occupy, and we are also active participants in projects to restore and improve the environment surrounding us. We support the aspirations of the Whanganui Iwi to seek the return of the river to their own guardianship."

As we sit, a number of friends and neighbors pulley across the river to stop in for a nosh and a chat. One of them is Niko Tangaroa, who runs a "cultural exchange" company called Waka Tours, and he offers to take Walker and me on a jet-boat ride up the river to an old marae.

The Whanganui is in spate, running large and brown, as though all the rivers of Aotearoa are tearing down this canyon. After the invite, Niko has second thoughts, wondering out loud if the idea is sage. But Walker has never been on a jet boat, and his enthusiasm is palpable. He is an active rafter and a great swimmer, so Niko, after reconsidering his reconsideration, says we'll give it a go.

As we trundle up the canyon to the put-in, Niko tells me that his late father, also named Niko Tangaroa, started the first Māori ecotourism venture in 1992 as a political vehicle. The water of the Whanganui River has always been sacred to the local Māori, but in the 1970s the government backed the Tongariro Power Scheme, which diverted the upper river to Lake Taupo, the freshwater lake the size of Singapore that smacks the center of the country. The scheme not only changed the nature and quality of the river, but it also reduced the water volume during certain times of year to the point that fish stocks were depleted. Niko says it altered a life force, taking away the mana of Māori who lived along the river and impacting the ability of local Māori to truly uphold kaitiakitanga. Now it is a river of tears.

Affected Māori fought to stop the scheme, but failed, and so Niko's father thought that if he started a company that would share the river, its history, its adventures, and its spirit with visitors, then he might be able to build a constituency with enough influence to correct the government's course.

In his father's lifetime it didn't work, and in some ways things got worse. The government sold concessions to outsiders to harvest river eels, the major food source for local Māori and the original serpents in this Eden. Herbicides leached into tributaries, then into the river itself. Hills were mowed down like grass to make way for "hoofed locusts" (John Muir's description of sheep) and cattle. Niko spent most of this period as a mechanical engineer in Perth, Australia, oblivious to what was happening along his heritage river. But with his father's passing, Niko came home, and in 2002 he took over the company. At that time, he says, he rediscovered his identity and values. He continues with his father's concept today. With gradual grace, Waka Tours is immersing visitors in the Whanganui River, connecting minds to spirits and eliciting support. At the core of the border war is a contest of opposing creeds. One supposes that man is superior to all in nature, and therefore the ecosystem must bend to human will. God is separate from nature, and nature is condemned by God. The sixth-day creation passage in Genesis states, "And God said, Let us make man in our image, after our likeness: and let them have dominion over the fish of the sea, and over the fowl of the air, and over the cattle, and over all the earth, and over every creeping thing that creepeth upon the earth." In the Abrahamic concept, land is a commodity that belongs to man.

The other viewpoint, a sort of Paleolithic moral order, holds that people are a component to the community of everything on earth—that the whole of existence is related, and therefore each element deserves respect and safeguarding. We are on equal footing with wakas, wekas, and wētās, the giant, flightless insects endemic to Aotearoa. We are family.

As we pile out of Niko's truck at the put-in, I see that someone has finger-painted in the dust on his back window: "Pimp My Waka." But the jet boat into which we climb is a pretty spartan affair: no enclosures, no awnings, no plush seats, no decals. However, it goes fast.

Niko hands us raincoats and pants, and I look to the threatening sky, dark as a plum. "They're not for rain," he says with a grin. We zip up and pile into the boat.

Before pushing off, Niko cuts a curling fern frond from the bank—the same koru shape that hangs around Ian's neck and adorns the tails of the Air New Zealand fleet, symbolizing new life, growth, and renewal—and places it in the bow. He next bows and recites a prayer for our safe passage up the raging waters. Then, in a soft pool of light, we push into a river angry-red with the blood of sediment and silt flushed by the rains of the past few days. The river flows quite fast at the edges, while in the deeper middle it bubbles up like thick porridge. The normal seethe and suck of the river is an audible roar, until the jet-boat engine starts. Then we are off, plowing upstream against the ferocity of a liquid army's charge, toward the menace of the Warrior Mountains.

In Māori mythology, the headwater mountains of Taranaki and Tongariro fought over the beautiful, bush-cloaked female mountain Pihanga. They argued and threw huge rocks at each other. They vented poisonous gases as they hissed and roared. They turned day to night by filling the sky with ash and smoke. Eventually, Tongariro emerged victorious and took his place next to Pihanga. Taranaki was heartbroken and plunged toward the setting sun, cutting a path to the coast, filling it with a river of tears: the Whanganui River, which today is overflowing with sobs.

We crash upward, adjusting the vectors and velocity, battling the surging, mixing, chocolate-brown waves. Long, thin, parallel masses of clouds break over us, a sign, Niko says, that the spirits are planting their

The koru *is the Māori name given to the newborn, unfurling fern frond and symbolizes new life, growth, strength and peace. It is an integral symbol in Māori carving and tattoos.*

kūmara. Then, suddenly, silver beads pock the river and draw a curtain around us. Spray stings our faces like BBs, and the banks seem to be melting with the flood.

Walker, my son, is lost in the dizziness of speed and hypersensation. It is easy to feel why jet boating can be so intoxicating.

Just as the rain begins to pound, we pull toward the left bank to an ancient, fortified pa, Tieke Kāinga. Some of Niko's relatives hail from here. Niko takes the fern that has traveled with us and places it on the ground, saying that the gesture is a symbol of how Māori of the Whanganui are woven together by the filaments of water, of how we are all interdependent. The Department of Conservation turned the knoll above our mooring into a tramping hut, but Niko's relatives, in an act of irredentism, have occupied the land since 1993 and continue to be involved in the legalities of a land claim. They have reconstructed a beautiful marae, with an elaborate totem pole, and bring tourists here to experience a *pōwhiri,* or welcome ceremony, followed by a communal meal.

Niko says strict protocols must be observed when visiting the marae. He has Walker and me sit on a bench in the rain. It is quiet, and in the flat light the raindrops look like silver threads, like static on an old film. The air seems thick enough to drink. I open my mouth and discover it is.

Then two women in feathered robes assemble in front of us and make what is called the *karanga,* the call to the visitors. Their voices sound not feminine or sirenlike, but rather like a composite of all Māori who have ever passed through this marae, combining their laughter and cries. The purpose of the call, Niko interprets, is to weave a metaphorical rope around the guests for safe passage. Then there is an *inoi* (prayer) to ensure the safety of the villagers and the proceedings. Next, from a fierce-looking male, comes a *wero,* a challenge, to determine our intentions. At last there is the *haka pōwhiri,* the welcome dance, meant to pull the spiritual canoe and the visitors into the marae, but unlike at rugby matches and tourist shows, here it is performed without urgency, as though underwater, with an underwritten grace that is more ethereal than thespian.

After the ritual and a feast of a hot lunch, we walk to the totem pole, which is carved with figurines of past kaitiaki of the river. The rain stops for a moment, and white butterflies hover like tiny ghosts. I can smell, I think, the lineal past wafting from the moist earth. A butterfly alights on my sleeve, folds and unfolds

The author about to embark down the river with his son, Walker Bangs

its wings a few beats, then floats away like a whisper and melts into the light. As we head back to the jet boat, Niko says that Walker and I are now part of his extended family—that we are now kaitiaki of this place.

As we board the boat, I look to the water's edge, where a colony of ferns glisten and dance as the current strokes the stems with fluid fingers. I look upriver to the warrior mountains and remember traveling through the next river valley in the mid-1990s. That trip is a mackled page in my existence now. I took a paddle down the Rangitaiki River, bordering the Uruwera Mountain Range, and flashed through some fifty rapids in a few hours. I hiked through Tongariro National Park, distinguished in many ways, but especially notable in that it allowed New Zealand to claim to be the second country in the world to establish a national park, following the United States with its designation of Yellowstone. It was also first in the world to achieve UNESCO World Heritage status for cultural values, thanks to its spiritual status among Māori. After my plucky adventures, I drove to the lakeside resort of Taupo, where I gave a presentation on U.S. adventure media to a hall of Kiwi outfitters. A tall, lanky man with a pioneer face—north-weathered, sinewy, and hollow, with a habit of flicking his eyes to the horizon as though searching for a distant mountain—approached me after the slide show and introduced himself as Himalayan guide Rob Hall. I knew of the legendary mountaineer, the guide with the stellar record of getting clients to the top of Everest, the cautious climber with the strict summit-day turnaround rule, the rival to American Scott Fischer, who ran Mountain Madness, an outfitter with which my own adventure company, Mountain Travel Sobek, sometimes booked "seven summit" clients. There was a vivid sense that Rob collaborated with forces behind the pageant of the ordinary world. Rob talked a bit about his upcoming Everest climb and an opportunity to entice *Outside* magazine writer Jon Krakauer, who was on assignment, to switch from Fischer's expedition to his own. I encouraged Rob to recruit Krakauer with a better offer, advising that a feature in *Outside* could do wonders for his business.

Ultimately, Krakauer did switch expeditions, joining Hall and his team on the fateful climb during which Rob himself lost his life, leaving his pregnant wife and the whole of the New Zealand climbing community to mourn. I have no idea whether I had any influence on that decision or whether things might have turned out differently had Krakauer remained with his original choice, Scott Fischer. There is no doubt in my mind, though, that Krakauer's presence as a media observer affected decisions and outcomes. Since Galileo, scientists have adopted the view that they are objective observers of the natural world. That was implicit in every aspect of their behavior, even the way they wrote such things in scientific papers as "it was observed…." For three hundred years, that impersonal quality was a hallmark of science, and it became the accepted rule of media. Scientists, writers, and reporters claimed to be objective, with the observer having little or no influence on the results.

But in the twentieth century, a different perspective evolved. Physicists now believe one cannot measure even a single subatomic particle without affecting it. If one inserts an instrument to measure a particle's position, the particle's velocity will change. If the velocity is measured, the position will change. This basic truth became the Heisenberg uncertainty principle: that whatever you study (or report on), you also change. In the case of the Everest expeditions of 1996, the act of observation may have altered the outcome severely, and I wondered for years whether I should feel any fault for a few words of advice.

SHEAR
MADNESS

He iti wai kowhao waka e tahuri te waka.

A little water through the lashing hole shipwrecks
the canoe.

Walker needs to head home after our little adventure, but I continue to Taupo with Ian once again showing the way. Ian is a constant emollient, always on his cell phone attempting to improve our quite fine itinerary. That seems a symptom of another Kiwi characteristic, what they call an "if it ain't broke, fix it anyway" spirit. He looks tired, though. I could travel across New Zealand for three weeks with the bags under his eyes. "She'll be right," he says, twinkling, with every unexpected turn, undaunted, ever with a smile like a curved blade.

We drive past cattle and sheep—lots of sheep. What Captain Cook wrought. He deposited the first sheep here during his second voyage in 1773, a ram and a ewe, both of which died munching unfamiliar, poisonous plants. The missionary Samuel Marsden had better luck: his flock took, and by the late 1840s, there were a hundred thousand sheep in New Zealand. The first refrigerated ship carried five thousand slaughtered sheep to Britain in 1882, and remoteness was removed from the equation.

Now there are some fifty million sheep, more than ten for every person. At one point, the government tried to impose a fart tax to raise money for research on cutting harmful emissions. The methane emitted by farm animals is responsible for more than half of New Zealand's greenhouse gases. But rural New Zealanders, as the constituency of the agrarian democracy that Jefferson once envisioned for America, raised a stink. The Federated Farmers of New Zealand started a campaign called FART (Fight Against Ridiculous Taxes) and beat back the initiative.

We stay the night at the Bayview Wairakei Resort ("Lake Taupo's premiere Conference and Holiday Resort"), about as eco as a Holiday Inn, with a "best surprise is no surprise" philosophy. It does have a nine-hole golf course and six spa pools. Taupo is the largest lake in Australasia, so big it's

The Wairakei Terraces. Once natural but then lost to diversion in a power scheme, they are back. A group of Māori whose ancestors used the thermal waters of the region for cooking, bathing, heating, and healing, as well as steaming their dead, have replicated the terraces with Disneyesque verisimilitude.

tidal. It is also the leisure epicenter of New Zealand, a place where people seek to relax, though its origins were as violent and cataclysmic as any on earth. About twenty-six thousand years ago, one of the world's biggest-ever eruptions left Lake Taupo as its crater. When the volcano blew again about AD 177, it was the most powerful and destructive eruption in historic times, almost ten times as powerful as Krakatau's eruption in 1883. Sunlight-filtering ash, pumice, and gases were blasted forty miles into the atmosphere, affecting global climate change (the earth and its oceans were cooler for several decades) and producing spectacular sunsets recorded by contemporaneous Chinese and Roman scribes.

With morning, we head across the road to the celebrated Wairakei Terraces in the heart of a valley called Waiora, which means "healthy water." Between the tendrils of steam and mist, we meet operator Jim Hill, who is ushering in tourists to a new and improved cauldron of attractions.

Jim hails from both worlds—his father is of European descent, his mother Māori—so he feels comfortable telling both sides of the story.

The European version of the origin of this place says the terraces were formed over thousands of years by a geyser that played over the slopes of Mount Tarawera. By the time of Pakeha settlement, the silica deposits rose like a giant white-and-pink wedding cake from the shores of Lake Rotomahana. Soon thereafter, the bizarre natural staircase became a major tourist attraction.

Māori, of course, have their own storied explanation. A well-regarded spiritual leader, Ngatoroirangi, made an early voyage to Aotearoa. He decided to explore inland and made his way to the eastern side of Lake Taupo, where he took a day to rest. When the clouds rolled away, he caught sight of the gleaming beauty of Mount Tongariro. Overwhelmed by its majesty, he decided to climb its summit. After traveling to its base, he ordered his companions to stay put while he and his slave, Aruhoe, climbed the peak. He said, "This is a hazardous venture, and if I am to return safely, you who remain must heed my words well. Eat no food. This will give me the strength I need, and the gods will stay with me. When I return, we will feast together, and I will tell you of the things I learn from the mountain."

The journey proved hazardous. The snowy air froze their breath and iced their fingers, numbed their toes and stiffened their joints. Aruhoe stumbled many times, but Ngatoroirangi urged him onward.

Looking across the harbor toward the town of Kaikoura and the Kaikoura Ranges beyond

Meanwhile, those waiting at the mountain's foot grew weary and hungry. "He may have perished and we wait in vain," said one. "Hunger is an impatient thing," said another. So, with sidelong glances at the mountain, they lit their cooking fires and ate. Their actions allowed the cold to drive its icy fingers into Ngatoroirangi's heart. He bent over in agony from the stabbing cold and prayed to his sisters in Hawaiki. "Send fire to warm me!' he cried. "Do not delay or I will surely perish. Come quickly. I am carried away by the cold south wind."

His sisters heard his prayer. They called to the fire demons Te Pupu and Te Hoata, who plunged into the sea and swam quickly until they came to Aotearoa. As they lifted their heads into the air, the earth burst into flames and became a volcano. They saw they still had many miles to go, so down they went once more into the seas, leaving a steaming, bubbling wake in their path.

At last, at Aotearoa, they surfaced again, but still short of the goal. They traveled and popped up again and again, creating volcanoes at each surfacing. Then, like a flash of lightning, the demons burst through the enormous pyramid of Tongariro, arriving as Ngatoroirangi lay on the edge of death.

Aruhoe had already died, but the volcanic heat created by the demons revived Ngatoroirangi. The warmth spread through his veins, sending life to his muscle and bone. After gaining his strength, Ngatoroirangi threw the body of Aruhoe into the crater. And so it is that thermal activity came to the region, and the descendants of Ngatoroirangi became the guardians.

But despite the guardianship, or perhaps because it was not fully observed, the gods or nature threw a temper tantrum.

In the early hours of June 10, 1886, Mount Tarawera erupted, sending smoke six miles high, burying three Māori villages in ash and

Across Lake Ohakuri are sulfur-crusted pits, gaseous bores, craters of boiling mud, and bubbling pools edged with beads of carbon dioxide.

lava, killing at least one hundred fifty people, and sending hundreds more fleeing for their lives.

Lake Rotomahana exploded with a boom heard for miles, spewing steam and mud for five hours, and then emptied like an unplugged sink. Turned upside down, the land reviewed itself. When the lake refilled, it grew to several times its original size, burying the terraces. Only bubbles and steam remained. And the stories.

One came from a guide named Sophia, daughter of a Māori mother and a Scottish father, who had found a satisfying career conducting tours of the fabled Pink and White Terraces, or Otukapuarangi ("fountain of the clouded sky") on the edges of Lake Rotomahana. They were at the time New Zealand's most famous tourist attraction. Ten days before the eruption, Sophia set out across the lake with a party of tourists on their way to the terraces. There were six Māori paddlers, three Māori women, and six Pakeha tourists. A little more than a mile out, they saw a war canoe approach, with some Māori paddling while others stood. Their bowed heads were crowned with feathers, emblems of death. The canoe moved closer, but then faded and disappeared. All with Sophia saw it, as did those in another tourist boat. Sophia and the Māori knew what it meant: it was a minatory message from the spirit world—a death warning from *atua,* the gods.

The explosion obliterated the terraces, but the warm waters themselves became a tourist hot spot. At the start of the twentieth century, the area's graduated pools were touted for their mystical healing powers and spa qualities, and people from around the world came for a soak and a salve. In 1901, the Department of Tourist and Health Resorts, the world's first government ministry for tourism, was established. In 1903, a government report proclaimed: "Cripples throw away their crutches and the gouty man regains his health."

But then the main bathing pool, Te Kiri o Hinekai, known later as the Honeymoon Pool, was closed in the 1960s when the stream was diverted during construction of the Wairakei Geothermal Power Development.

Now, a group of Māori whose ancestors used the thermal waters of the region for cooking, bathing, heating, and healing, as well as steaming their dead, have replicated the terraces with Disneyesque verisimilitude. Pouring silica-rich wastewater piped from the geothermal power plant over concrete steps, they've re-created what nature and then man took away, and tapped into a new tourism vein.

Māori believe that our mana (our integrity, our spiritual strength) is housed within our heads. We earn our mana throughout our lives, and it is acknowledged through the respect with which people treat us or the respect that we demand from others. Because of this, Māori consider a person's head *tapu,* or sacred. When a great warrior or chief would fall in battle, the enemy might behead the victim and consume the contents of the head in order to steal the mana. To prevent that, the fallen warrior's tribe would behead him first, burying the rest of the body but throwing the head into the steaming-hot pool where no enemy could get to it.

At the re-created terraces, the feel of simulacrum and the perfume of rotten eggs are in the air. An artificial geyser pours superheated water, swirling with the crystallized residue of blue, pink, orange, and white minerals, in a cascade over the twenty-foot-high terraces. A "mystical" walkway, artfully appointed with carvings, curves around the spectacle, and a mechanical tiki mask pops up every few minutes like something in a haunted house. Other decoctions include a pool that claims therapeutic powers, a foot bath, an animal park, and a house featuring Māori carvers and weavers at work. In the evenings, an Off-Broadway–type show features burly Māori men dressed as minstrel warriors doing the big-eyed, tongue-poking haka while Māori maids swing poi balls and sing songs.

Jim Hill is the CEO of NETCOR (New Zealand Education and Tourism Corporation), the privately owned concern that did the deal with the thermal plant and developed the modern Wairakei Terraces. He says, "The thermal power here is a gift. We call ourselves kaitiaki today. There is no reason why everybody can't be kaitiaki as we go through into life."

At this point the concept of kaitiakitanga seems almost real, attainable, like a fish shimmering beneath the surface of shallow water, until I ask Jim to share some of the culture he offers in the park. He leads me to an overlook with steam churning from a blue pool and introduces me to Haromi Koopu, a *kaumatua,* or respected elder, of the local

Tuwharetoa tribe. Today, she sports a *kahukiwi,* a cloak of chicken feathers, a replica of one her ancestors wore that was woven with kiwi feathers. With elegiac ardor and uncommon grace, she breaks into a song in Te Reo Māori and then sings the English translation: "Love is the key to everything we do, and Jesus is the source of it all."

After exploring the show of Wairakei, Ian offers to show me the real deal, the freak of nature known as The Hidden Valley of Orakei Korako (place of adorning). It lies about half an hour down a twisting road rich with expression—hotheaded and encased by ignimbrite cliffs.

The only way to reach this spectacle is by a brief boat ride across Lake Ohakuri, created by a dam slung across the Waikato River in 1961. Once here, though, it is like stepping into a dinosaur diorama—and that's not a unique observation. Scenes of the BBC TV natural-history series *Walking with Dinosaurs* were filmed here among the sulfur-crusted pits, gaseous bores, craters of boiling mud, and bubbling pools edged with beads of carbon dioxide. There are thirty-five active geysers and a hundred or so hot springs, as well as some of the largest sinter terraces in the world. (Outside this region, geysers appear in only a handful of places, including southwest Iceland and Yellowstone National Park.) Dinosaurs walked here sixty-five million years ago, and the impression is that not much has changed, though in fact much has, most of it in the last blink of time. The hydroelectric scheme that created Lake Ohakuri raised the water level some sixty feet, destroying two-thirds of the active area and swallowing a current's life. Two hundred hot springs and some seventy geysers were flooded. The Emerald Terrace, the largest geothermal terrace in New Zealand, was partially drowned.

Local Māori fought the dam but lost, and a wonder of the world was sent to a watery grave, like Atlantis. Today, eleven power stations—two geothermal, one coal and gas, and eight hydropower—line the banks of the Waikato River and provide 7 percent of New Zealand's electricity.

Now it is quiet here, save for the fizzing and burping, and Māori have settled in ushering tourists and telling stories. But just as I am to leave for the boat, a bubble in a blue pool next to my foot globs to the surface, a delicate effervescence that in a tiny way troubles the calm.

It was due east of Taupo at a curving coastline called Poverty Bay that Captain Cook made first footfall on New Zealand's friable soil on October 7, 1769. Local folklore tells that Māori perceived the *Endeavour* as an enormous bird with wings of great size and beauty, though first contact was less than fine-looking. Because of a misinterpretation of the traditional Māori challenge, Cook's men attacked and killed six local Māori in a reversal of fortune from Tasman's first encounter. The violence notwithstanding, Māori were intrigued with Cook and his exotic tools. Cook gave an iron nail to a small boy, who kept it all his life. As an old man and a chief, Horeta Te Taniwha recalled the magic moment:

"When our old men saw the ship, they said it was an **atua,** *a god, and the people on board were* tupua, *strange beings or goblins. . . . As our old men looked at the manner in which they came on shore, the rowers pulling with their backs to the bows of the boat, the old people said, 'Yes, it is so: these people are goblins; their eyes are at the back of their heads; they pull on shore with their backs to the land. . . .' As we did not know their language, we laughed. . . ."*

Violence was a cross-cultural currency for some time. In 1808, the British chaplain Samuel Marsden, lamenting his difficulty recruiting missionaries, wrote: "The character of the New Zealanders was considered more barbarous than that of any other savage nation, so that few would venture out to a country where they could anticipate nothing less than to be killed and eaten by the natives." But a year later, a Captain Park of the English whaler *New Zealander* sailed to New Zealand with a flotilla of two hundred men. They killed Māori indiscriminately, burnt their houses, and destroyed their crops.

The most infamous incident, however, was the 1809 *Boyd* massacre.

The *Boyd* was a 395-ton brigantine convict ship that sailed from Sydney Cove to Whangaroa on the east coast of Northland Peninsula in New Zealand in October 1809 under the command of Captain John Thompson. It carried about seventy passengers.

Aboard was George, the son of a Māori chief from Whangaroa. He asked to work for his passage on the vessel, but once on board he refused to obey certain orders, claiming that he had bad health and was the son of a chief. He was flogged twice.

On reaching Whangaroa, where the *Boyd* was to pick up spars cut from kauri trees, George reported the indignities he had been subjected to and showed the marks on his back where he had been whipped. Māori formed a plan for *utu* (revenge).

Three days after the arrival, Māori invited Captain Thompson to follow their canoes up the harbor and into a forest to find kauri trees that could be used for spars. Thompson set off with his chief officer and three men, following the Māori canoes to the entrance of the Kaeo River.

The remaining crew members stayed aboard the ship with the passengers, preparing for an intended journey to England.

The Māori utu plan, led by Tipahi, began when the canoes and longboats were out of sight of the *Boyd*.

When the boats reached the riverbank, Māori pulled weapons from their cloaks and attacked the Pakeha, killing all with clubs and axes.

One group of Māori then carried the bodies to their village to be cooked and eaten. The other group waited until dusk before manning a longboat.

At nightfall, the longboat slipped alongside the *Boyd,* where it was greeted by the remaining crew members. Secretly, many canoes filled with Māori were awaiting the signal to attack.

The first blow was an ax to the head of an officer. The attackers then crept around the deck, killing the crew quietly. One of the Māori then called the passengers to the deck. A woman was the first of the passengers to be killed.

Five survivors hid among the rigging up the mast, where they remained until daybreak. They watched in silent horror as the bodies of their shipmates were dismembered below them on the deck.

Sometime in midmorning, the survivors saw a large canoe enter the harbor. It belonged to Chief Te Pahi from the Bay of Islands, who had come to trade. The survivors called out to be saved.

The Whangaroa Māori watched as Te Pahi gathered the survivors aboard his canoe. The chief ordered his canoe to head for shore, but two canoes belonging to the attackers followed.

The survivors fled along the beach after scrambling ashore. Te Pahi watched helplessly as all but one were caught and killed by natives.

There were other survivors, initially spared. They included Ann Morley and her baby, who were found in a cabin; Thomas Davis, the ship's cabin boy, who had hidden in the hold; the second mate; and Betsy Broughton, a two-year-old girl.

Betsy was taken by a local chief, who put a feather in her hair and kept her for three weeks before rescue came. The mate was killed when his usefulness in making fishhooks ran out.

The Māori towed the *Boyd* toward their pa until it became grounded in mudflats. They spent several days ransacking the ship, tossing flour, salted pork, and bottles of wine overboard. They were, however, interested in a large cache of muskets and gunpowder.

About twenty Māori smashed open barrels of gunpowder and tried to get the muskets working. Chief Piopio tried one of the flints, which sparked and ignited the gunpowder, blowing up the ship.

Piopio and nine other Māori were killed instantly.

All that was left of the *Boyd* was a burnt-out hull. A Māori *tapu* (declaration of a place as sacred or taboo) was placed on the ship.

Altogether, the Māori killed sixty-six Pakeha in the incident. The survivors were saved by the arrival of the ship *The City of Edinburgh,* which went to Whangaroa under Alexander Berry after hearing of the massacre. Berry rescued four, including the mother and daughter and the cabin boy. Crew members found piles of human bones on the shoreline, many clearly showing teeth marks.

Berry also captured two Māori chiefs responsible for the massacre, but after threatening them with death and securing the ship papers of the *Boyd,* he released them as slaves rather than chiefs. His clemency avoided further bloodshed, inevitable if he had executed the men, but acts of violence from all quarters continued for decades, and for a time New Zealand enjoyed the reputation as the most dangerous place in the Pacific. It still has that reputation in some quarters, but not for its bloodshed; rather, for its ideas.

MAN BITES PLANET

He taonga nō te whenua me hoki anō ki te whenua.

What is given by the land should return to the land.

F rom the caldera of Taupo, we head north again, into the greater drama of wind, heat, and light, the world unfolding in time, to Auckland, the city with the largest Polynesian population in the world. In the 1960s, the New Zealand government made an immigration outreach to Pacific Islanders to build up its wan work force, and it worked.

I book into the Heritage, a place recommended by my old friend Tom Peirce. Tom told a story that stayed with me about an incident at the Heritage. Tom's family used to own the Selway Lodge in Idaho, and one day Tom's mother, Freddie, was invited by a rafting operator friend to join a float down the Selway River. She accepted and found herself seated in the raft next to Sir Edmund Hillary, with whom she bonded as they ran the rapids together. They became good friends and stayed in touch after the trip. Years later, Tom was escorting an alumni group from Stanford, and they booked into the Heritage. Tom, who had never met Ed Hillary, decided to give him a call. He reached the legend, who picked up his own phone, which was the first surprise. Tom introduced himself as Freddie's son and sheepishly invited him to the hotel to meet with his group. Tom recalled it was like inviting a rock star to pop over, and rock stars don't usually countenance a fan's overtures for social interface. To Tom's astonishment, Hillary accepted and made his way to the Heritage to join the group for dinner, and the evening was remembered as epic.

The Heritage is a converted Art Deco–era department store, now a luxury hotel but with a twist that is perhaps indicative of the shifting sands: like the city of Kaikoura and more than one hundred other tourism operations throughout New Zealand, the Heritage is benchmarked by Green Globe for sustainability, pledging to monitor and improve its energy conservation, reduction of waste, and efficient use of resources.

The property features two heated swimming pools, two spa pools, a sauna, and a floodlit tennis court, so it faces some atonement on the eco-front, but the point of benchmarking is to set a baseline and commit to improvements. There are water-flow reducers in the rooms, recycled phone books, energy-saving lamps, key tag switches (which activate power to a room when a guest inserts the electronic room key and cut off power when a departing guest removes the key), water-based paint on the walls, and a riot of live plants around the lobby floor. The goodness doesn't prevent a false fire alarm, sounded by devices with mercury-free batteries, that has all the guests spilling into the street for a delightful exercise in mutual gawking at various states of dishabille.

While in the city, I decide I must stop at Air New Zealand to explore how the national carrier for a country that is trying to become a world model of environmental consciousness and policy deals with the fact that a great number of its visitors must take very long flights to get here. How can an international airline be a viable business and attempt to achieve Prime Minister Helen Clark's goal of countrywide carbon neutrality?

During the taxi ride to Fanshawe Street, I ask the cabbie about the emerging ethos of kaitiakitanga and how it is affecting life in Auckland. He shakes his head in disgust and says, "Quite a few things slow down progress here."

A few years ago, a major road-construction project was stopped because local Māori complained that the work was upsetting Karu Tahi, a fabled water monster, who lived in a bog in the path of the proposed highway. Such is the influence of Māori mythology today. When the beast is hungry, it's easy to slip glass into its diet.

I carry some psychic weight as I head into the Air New Zealand lobby. It has nothing to do with carbon footprints or environmental standards. Nonetheless, it haunts me still, and staring at an old picture of a McDonnell Douglas DC-10-30 sends shivers through me.

Beginning in the late 1970s, the adventure company I founded, Sobek, started featuring trips to New Zealand, and I started working with the Air New Zealand district sales manager in Los Angeles, Paul Klassovity. We published a joint brochure on adventures in New Zealand, one of the first for the American market, which we both distributed through our various channels and partners. We enjoyed some success, and a friendship blossomed. Paul was an adventurer himself, and I invited him to join me rafting on the American River near our offices. After that, we talked about sharing more adventures around the world.

In the fall of 1979, Paul called me to pitch a unique tour that Air New Zealand had devised, a scenic day flight over Antarctica that departed from Auckland. That piqued my interest because we had just started to offer trips by boat to Antarctica, and they were proving popular but long and expensive. Paul then said he had agreed to join a departure and asked if I would join him. He said Ed Hillary would be on board as well, acting as a guide.

I was sorely tempted by the offer, but it conflicted with another project into which I was deeply immersed, an expedition to make the first descent of the Indus River in Pakistan. I told Paul I had to pass but hoped I could make a later flight. I was sorry to miss an adventure like this with both Paul and Ed Hillary on board. I wished Paul good luck and said we should get together as soon as he got back to compare notes and plot the future of adventure.

Air New Zealand Flight 901 took off on November 28, 1979, heading south, carrying 20 crew members and 237 passengers, but not Ed

Hillary, who had canceled, citing other commitments. Instead, his long-time friend and climbing companion Peter Mulgrew stood in as guide.

Captain Jim Collins and copilot Greg Cassin had never flown to Antarctica, but they were experienced pilots, and the flight was considered a simple one. They input the coordinates into the plane's computer before the departure at 8:21 a.m. The flight was supposed to arrive back in Auckland at 6:09 p.m. Unbeknownst to them, however, the coordinates had been modified earlier that morning to correct an error introduced years previously and undetected until then. The new coordinates changed the flight plan so that the plane would fly twenty-eight miles east of where the pilots intended to fly. The coordinates instructed the plane to fly over not McMurdo Sound, but rather Lewis Sound—and directly over Mount Erebus, a 12,448-foot volcano.

After about four hours, the flight was forty-two miles from McMurdo Station, where the radio communications center allowed the pilots to descend to 10,000 feet and to continue "visually." Collins believed the plane was over flat, low ground.

Collins then told McMurdo Station that he would be dropping farther, to 2,000 feet, at which point he switched control of the aircraft to the computer system. As bad luck would have it, at the time there was a layer of cloud that blended with the white of the volcano, forming a sector whiteout. There was no visual contrast between the two.

At 12:49 p.m., the ground proximity warning system began sounding an alarm that the plane was dangerously close to terrain. Although Collins immediately called for maximum engine power, there was no time for either Collins or Cassin to divert the aircraft, and eleven seconds after the warning began blaring, the plane plowed into the side of

The township of Kaikoura sits on a siltstone peninsula that juts out from the snow-collared Seaward Kaikoura Ranges, a spur of the Southern Alps, and according to legend was carved out by a Māori god with a magic sword.

Mount Erebus and disintegrated, instantly killing all on board, including twenty-two Americans and my friend Paul Klassovity.

Today that accident could not happen, because all major passenger aircraft carry EGPWS (enhanced ground proximity warning system), a digital map readout of virtually all the earth's terrain that gives ample warning of impending obstacles.

After being issued a security badge, I head up in the elevator to a conference room to meet Ed Sims, group general manger of Air New

198

Zealand. I begin by asking him the amount of emissions I contributed to the atmosphere on my Air New Zealand flight from Los Angeles to Auckland. He says that the airline has calculated carbon dioxide emissions at about a ton per passenger per 6,500 miles, the flight distance between the two cities. And that in terms of carbon offsets against this footprint, planting one large, fast-growing tree, such as a Monterey pine, would compensate for this over twenty-eight years. I am suddenly dizzy with guilt, thinking my various flights have caused my body to move faster than my soul. I am responsible for a ton of emissions into the atmosphere just from flying here this trip, and I've traveled here a few times.

Ed then pulls out a PowerPoint he is going to present to his staff in the afternoon called "Let's Clear the Air." It says the airline has a three-part approach to the issue of global warming: acknowledge, measure, reduce. He says that the debate about climate change is over and that being defensive is pointless. Airlines pollute, contributing about 2 percent of global carbon dioxide emissions a year. The plane truth is that Air New Zealand consumes more than 8 million barrels of fuel per year and is responsible for emitting about 3.6 million tons of carbon dioxide, more than 90 percent from burning jet fuel, the rest mostly from using electricity for offices, bases, and such.

Ed also acknowledges that the greatest selling point for potential visitors to New Zealand is the pristine environment (the ad campaign from Tourism New Zealand is "100% Pure New Zealand"), so the national carrier needs to come as close as possible to being a clean, green machine. Therefore, the airline now makes gliding descents, uses electric power rather than auxiliary jet power when parked, and has reduced its flight weight by moving to electronic onboard documents and cutting back on soda cans and other drink and food items. (Two Coke cans cost about NZ $400 in fuel a year.) The carrier uses a citrus-based, environmentally friendly engine cleaner. The company is also investing in research on exotic fuel alternatives, such as an algae-derived bio-jet-fuel blend, and is developing a carbon-offsetting program. It has ordered a new fleet of Boeing Dreamliner 787s, due in 2010, that will achieve a further 20 percent gain in fuel efficiency, which is not only good for the environment, but also good business.

One of the issues Air New Zealand, like the whole of the country, has to face is the current movement to "eat local" rather than consume food that needs to travel long distances to get to a dining table. In Europe, there is a push for "food miles labeling" so consumers can count miles as they might calories, thereby feeling they are lessening their carbon footprints. This is an especially worrisome issue for a country remote to most of the world that rings up more than NZ$5 billion a year exporting its signature lamb and beef.

On its face, the connection between reducing food miles and decreasing greenhouse-gas emissions is a no-brainer. But some here argue that the issue exemplifies the vividness heuristic: the tendency to give undue weight to a particularly vivid or newsworthy example. Researchers at Lincoln University in New Zealand recently published a study challenging the premise that more food miles automatically mean greater fossil-fuel consumption.

It all depends, the study suggests, on how the carbon calculator is brandished. Instead of measuring a product's carbon footprint through food miles alone, the Lincoln University scientists expanded the equations to include other energy-consuming aspects of production—what economists call "factor inputs and externalities"—such as water use, harvesting techniques, fertilizer outlays, renewable-energy applications, means of transportation (and the kind of fuel used), amount of carbon dioxide absorbed during photosynthesis, disposal of packaging, storage procedures, and dozens of other production-related inputs.

Incorporating these measurements into their evaluations, scientists reached some counterintuitive conclusions. They found that lamb raised on New Zealand's clover-choked pastures and shipped 11,000 miles by boat to Britain produced 1,520 pounds of carbon dioxide emissions per ton while British lamb produced 6,280 pounds of carbon dioxide per ton, in part because inferior British pastures force farmers to use supplemental feed. In other words, it is four times as energy-efficient for Londoners to buy lamb imported from the other side of the world as to buy it from a producer in their backyard. Similar results were found for dairy products and fruit, including the Chinese gooseberry, better known today as the kiwi fruit.

These life-cycle measurements are causing environmentalists worldwide to rethink the logic of food miles. New Zealand's most prominent environmental-research organization, Landcare Research–Manaaki Whenua, explains that localism "is not always the most environmentally sound solution if more emissions are generated at other stages of the product life cycle than during transport." New Zealanders, more than most of the rest of the world, know that the tyranny of geography is often a myth, and that distance is not the enemy of awareness.

When I get back to my hotel, I decide to send Ed Sims an e-mail thanking him for his time. His response comes back with a header I have not seen to this point: "Please consider the environment before printing this e-mail."

THE PRIME TRUTH

Kāhore a te rākau nei whakaaro; kei te tohunga te whakaaro.

The block of wood has no understanding; such insight belongs to the skillful carver.

t seems that if there is a bead to be gotten on what is happening in the big picture of New Zealand I need to go to the top. So I call the office of the prime minister and request an interview. As it turns out, the Right Honourable Helen Clark is coming through Auckland on her way back from a European conference, and she agrees to a chat.

So we get together at the offices of Tourism New Zealand and sit on an orange couch for a wide-ranging discussion. I learn that Helen, who hails from a sheep and cattle farm, is quite the adventurer: She has climbed Kilimanjaro and made it up to just shy of twenty thousand feet on Aconcagua in Argentina, and has backcountry-skied in North America. She loves the great outdoors and has sampled many of the adventures of her own country, from rafting to tramping to ice climbing. And she loves to watch the Discovery Channel. We find we are the same age and have both been involved in the political ructions and antiwar rallies of the 1960s, and environmental activism thereafter. After the pleasantries, I ask about her bold statements proposing that New Zealand be the first carbon-neutral country in the world. With the tongue-and-groove precision of someone who machines her thoughts to the finest hairbreadth precision, she tells me it is an achievable aspiration "if we really set our minds to it."

I ask if there is something about the Kiwi character that makes this so, and she posits: "In our self-image we see ourselves as clean and green. My challenge is to make sure we have real substance behind that. We feel it in our bones, but we're going to have to prove it to the world, and we need to go the extra mile to show that we're sustainable."

What are New Zealand's goals in terms of carbon neutrality?

"I've set New Zealand a challenge to aspire to be the world's first truly sustainable nation. Now that's a challenge as it would be for any country.... But we have it within in our power for example to have the base load of our energy generation drawn entirely from renewable sources and to push the fossil fuel, coal generation, into the reserve supply. We have it in our capacity to have much better public transportation and more people using it. We have it in our capacity to have much more effective waste strategies—for every household and business to commit to sustainability at their own level."

Why is New Zealand hoping to do this first? Why are you taking the lead in terms of the world's nations?

"We're convinced that in the twenty-first century, being sustainable will mean prosperity. And you won't be prosperous without being sustainable. Consumers now are very discerning. They want to know about the product. They want to know how it's produced, where it comes from, its life cycle. This is true for food, but also travel. People are really worried by what's happening to the global environment. Who would have thought, even five years ago, that the Davos World Economic Summit would be dominated by the climate-change and sustainability debate? These issues are now critical. And In New Zealand, we like to be part of solving the world's problems, and we believe we can lead by example on these issues."

Where I come from, in some quarters, politicians believe it's not worth it because there's such a cost. They say it's too expensive.

"We believe you won't be prosperous without being environmentally sound because people aren't going to want to buy from you if they see you as a dirty producer from a dirty country. In fact, the next round of protectionism could well be based on trade barriers put around such

The lakes of Aotearoa are filled with the tears of the gods.

countries and such products. It's a question for us as to how we get ourselves on the best footing for the twenty-first century. Partly it's about economic survival, but it's also about ensuring that our economic survival is consistent with survival of the planet. If we don't arrest a lot of the bad trends that are out there of the negative impact that we human beings are having on the environment, it's not going to be much of a world to leave our grandchildren and great-grandchildren."

How do you expect New Zealand to influence government policies of other countries in terms of climate change?

"I think we're going to start to see countries becoming quite competitive in what they do to meet these challenges. Just as some companies are."

Is New Zealand's size an advantage?

"Because New Zealand is small, it can often do things that others can't. Ideas move fast here. We're all just a few degrees removed from one another. So we have an opportunity to pioneer things. Often, people come here and say, 'How did they do that? They're ahead of us?' We were the first country in the world where women gained the right to vote [in 1893], first to introduce industrial conciliation and arbitration, first to have public worker housing, among the first to have old-age pensions. We've pioneered a lot of things in New Zealand."

Why do people travel such long distances to visit New Zealand?

"People come to New Zealand looking for what their own country has lost, sometimes hundreds or even thousands of years ago. We have a biodiversity not replicated anywhere else in the world. We have a primeval world long since disappeared in other places. And people come for the people here. You can go to a country that is beautiful, but the people are horrible. You come here, and the country is beautiful, but the people are nice, too."

What about the culture?

"We have to apply the concept of sustainability across the four pillars: culture, environment, economy, and society. New Zealand is a little country—only 4.1 million people—so if we don't make superhuman efforts to sustain and promote our culture, we will be swamped by globalized culture and media."

What would you say is the spirit of New Zealand?

"Well, it is a spirit of community. We all help each other. But increasingly it is also a spirit of coexistence with nature. We come from a past where we cut things down and dug things up, and left quite a heavy footprint. Even so, because we were relatively recently settled, we were able to arrest that in time. That's why we have so much unspoiled land and coastline. And it's important to keep it that way."

How do you see indigenous philosophies, such as the Māori notion of kaitiakitanga, influencing the course of First World countries?

"I think this idea of guardianship is very, very important—that each of us has a responsibility to the earth of which we live. The key message is: Don't go into protecting your environment and becoming sustainable with the mind-set that this is going to cost you a whole lot of money. Go in with the mind-set that if you don't do this, it's going to endanger your way of life and the legacy you leave for future generations. We have it in our power to maintain our living standards in a First World country like New Zealand because we're sustainable. If we're not, our future is really quite bleak. So there's no choice. This is not a cost; this is an opportunity, and it's a challenge."

New Zealand is very rich in legends and myths, but is there a myth about New Zealand that you would like to dispel?

"There are myths that stop our story, such as that we are just a beautiful country with lots of sheep. We are a beautiful country with lots of sheep, but we are so much more: a place with unique cultures, unique outdoor environments, with lively arts, and a country that is on the forefront of things that are good. Come here, and you find people who are doing their best to make a difference. "

chapter twenty-six

STOP MAKING SENSE

He wahi rīriki noa nei tō tātou ao, nō te ao marama.

Our world is only a small part of the universe.

We still have a ways to travel to reach the far north of New Zealand, so we once again hit the road, narrow and rutted in these parts. I wonder if the rumble I feel is just the vehicle jarring up and down the hills, or is it kaitiakitanga stirring?

If coils of thought and policies have radiated to the rest of the world from this small country, it might make sense that ripples have touched the shores of the mother country. Just last year, Britain's Prince Charles received a Global Environmental Citizen Award from the Harvard Medical School's Center for Health and the Global Environment. He flew on a commercial flight to accept it, and at the dais he said: "We have come to see ourselves as being outside of nature, free to manipulate and control her constituent parts, imagining somehow that the whole will not suffer and can take care of itself, and of us, whatever we do." He went on to say that most urbanites today experience nature only through television, something to be switched on or off at will, and as a result many have lost a "sense of harmony." And he concluded by heralding the wisdom of indigenes who remain close to nature. "They consider themselves participants in it and define life on earth as 'sacred presence.' … They also take direct responsibility for the future."

Up to Kerikeri we wend by the Bay of Islands, where some 144 islands float within thirty miles of the coast. We check into the Stone Store Lodge, built and run by former dairy farmer Richard Miller. It sits on a palisade by an ancient pa that was called "The Mouth of War," overlooking the maw of the Kerikeri Inlet. It's where some of the first Pakeha put down their roots. Down past the gardens is New Zealand's oldest standing European building, dating to the 1820s, and the namesake stone store, a missionary granary built in 1836. Before opening the Stone Store, Richard took time to sail around the South Pacific, and after sampling a raft of potential ecoto-pias he decided the Bay of Islands best fit his vision for an organic, high-end homestay lodge. After our late check-in, Richard treats us to his thin-crust goat's cheese pizza, prepared in his outdoor, wood-fired oven. Richard is a member of an organic-garden group, and all the vegetable and fruit garnish-es are fresh and local—nothing carried by Air New Zealand.

The Bay of Islands is now a place of peace and equipoise, an ideal site for an eco-lodge. But it was not always so. It was the beachhead for the three scourges of Europe: prostitution, disease, and Christianity.

Charles Darwin set foot here in 1835 and was so enchanted he wrote in his journal: "This is not a pleasant place. Amongst the natives there is absent that charming simplicity which is found in Tahiti; and the greater part of the English are the very refuse of society."

Suites of disease took hold in the deadliest way. Māori fell to influ-enza, smallpox, measles, typhoid, cholera, whooping cough, and venereal diseases. These scourges spread from the Bay of Islands to the rest of the country and ultimately reduced the total Māori population by maybe two-fifths. What the original Māori had done to an innocent land was now being done to them.

Missionaries introduced their own poisons, including such peculiar notions as the idea that Māori were descended from the lost tribes of Israel. In the first twenty years of proselytizing, three missionar-ies were dismissed, one for adultery, one for drunkenness, and, according to one record, one "for a crime worse than either." Māori showed little interest in heeding the gospel, and one great chief, Hongi Hika, told his people that Christianity was not suitable for warriors. One of the first mis-sionaries, Thomas Kendall, ended up being converted by those he meant

Tāne Mahuta, "Lord of the Forest," named for a god in the Māori pantheon. Though not long ago there were many kauri trees bigger than Tāne Mahuta, they were all cut or burned, and so today this tower holds the record at 169 feet in height and 45 feet in circumference.

to convert. He would write: "I have been so poisoned with the apparent sublimity of their ideas that I have been almost completely turned from a Christian to a Heathen." Today, the reemergence and sublimity of some of the Māori ideas are resonating across all races and religions and throughout the length and breadth of the country.

The next morning, we make the short drive across the tail of upper New Zealand. There seems a sympathy between animate and inanimate here. As we drive, there sometimes appears an interchange of forms: a rock becomes a root, a sheep melts into a stone, a hill becomes a hut. There is so much illusion here. Like the shadows in a cave, figments can seem more real than reality itself.

The largest area of mature kauri forest is the Waipoua Forest, set aside for protection in 1952 and holding about three-quarters of New Zealand's remaining kauri.

We drive to the Waipoua Forest, sometimes called "The Dinosaur Forest," and there in a small car park we meet a gnomic man with a twinkly bearing, a hair vest, and bare feet. He is tree conservationist Stephen King. Concourses of flies buzz around this little patch, and while I swat, Stephen just revels in the attention. "It's like what the frog said: 'Time's fun when you're having flies.'"

Stephen, who is built close to the ground, made a name for himself in the 1970s when he squatted high up in a giant tōtara tree in the Pureora Forest in protest against the logging of native woodlands. He dared the bulldozers to advance, and won. The government ordered the felling stopped.

Now he is involved in the protection of the last great kauri trees and is a founding trustee of the Waipoua Forest Trust a partnership with the local Māori community that is working to extend the boundaries of the Waipoua Forest.

The kauri tree is a symbol for the country where it uniquely grows. A conifer, it is the largest by volume of any tree in the country, standing up to one hundred eighty feet tall in the emergent layer above the forest's main canopy. Kauri are so big that in the late 1800s, an entire family, two parents and thirteen children, set up home in one.

Kauri trees once blanketed the North Island, but not many are left standing. About a third of the kauri forests were burned by Māori. Then came the Europeans, who did the greatest ravage, using two-man crosscut saws in an orgy of felling. The kauri's strength and size made it a popular wood for construction and shipbuilding. It was particularly favored for top masts of European sailing ships because of its parallel grain and the absence of branches for much of its height. Its beautiful cognac color made it a favorite for ornamental wood paneling as well as high-end furniture. In the late nineteenth and early twentieth centuries, kauri gum was a valuable commodity for varnish, denture molds, and gilt edging on books. Today, most of the great kauri are gone: just 1 percent of New Zealand's old-growth forest remains.

The small remaining pockets of kauri forest have survived in areas not subjected to burning by Māori settlers and too inaccessible for European loggers. The largest area of mature kauri forest is the Waipoua Forest, set aside for protection in 1952 and holding about three-quarters of New Zealand's remaining kauri. (That might change with programs such as Trees for Travellers; the tree I planted was a kauri.)

Stephen takes me for a hike into the forest, sans shoes—he says he can feel the forest that way and gets a free foot massage every day—a homunculus on the humus. He points out several kauri, distinctive because of their oily bark, which look almost like the skin of a whale. In fact, Māori regard both the kauri and the sperm whale as *rangatira* (chiefs) of their respective realms and believe the two have a spiritual connection. The kauri gum is like the ambergris found in the intestines of the whale, but it is their unusual inversion of epidermis that inspired tales of the nexus.

The story goes that a long time ago, a sperm whale came ashore and spoke to the kauri: "Kauri! Come with me to the sea, which is fresh and cool."

"No!" said the kauri. "You may like the sea, but I prefer to stand here with my feet in the soil."

"All right," said the whale, "then let us agree to exchange our skins."

So that is why the bark of the kauri is thin and full of resinous oil, and why the skin on the back of the sperm whale, unlike the smooth skin of most other large whales, is knobby and treelike.

We curve around a fern-lined path to the base of a towering Doric column of a tree: Tāne Mahuta, "Lord of the Forest," named for a god in the Māori pantheon. Though not long ago there were many kauri trees bigger than Tāne Mahuta, they were all cut or burned, and so today this tower holds the record at 169 feet in height and 45 feet in circumference. It is, Stephen says, the largest rain forest tree on earth. There is no proof of the tree's age, but some estimate it to be middle-aged for a kauri, more than two thousand years old, which would mean that it sprouted before the birth of Christ and was a thousand years old when the first Māori set foot on Aotearoa. Time seeps like sap here.

"This tree is our identity as New Zealanders," Stephen says, "and the native forest here symbolizes New Zealand.

Time seeps like sap here. Some kauri trees are more than two thousand years old, having sprouted before the birth of Christ.

"If you look up in his branches, you'll see heaps of things growing; there's a whole forest of stuff up there."

My neck cranes back to take in the frenzy of static movement that makes up the high boughs. Those limbs are busy with moss, lichens, epiphytes, and a nimbus of other green things.

"There are more species living in this tree than you'll find in a whole redwood forest, including the world's smallest orchid. The theme of this rain forest is intimacy and diversity. That's the way the boss made it."

Tāne Mahuta looks like the boy dream of a perfect tree for a tree fort and seems to taunt the visitor to try a climb, but a wooden fence keeps amateur arborists at bay. Stephen insists he is not a kaitiaki—he says only Māori can inhabit that concept—but he is a guardian of Tāne Mahuta and as such climbs it twice a year to monitor its health and to collect seeds, which he plants in hopes of re-creating the bearing and breadth of the kauri forests.

Bay of Islands, where some 144 islands float within thirty miles of the coast.

"Every area in nature needs a guardian," Stephen says in his koan-like way. "Humans are put here to be stewards of what God has given them, not takers. When we plant seedlings in the ground, they take five hundred years to grow, but when they grow, how magical will it be?"

Stephen does not controvert the assertion that Māori devastated much of this forest, but believes that after a couple of hundred years, they found the right balance, and that their cosmology reflects that equilibrium. Europeans followed the same path. They blithely mowed down the forests, but now, after almost two hundred years, they too are discovering and endorsing balance. But balance comes with a cost. There is no logging of native forest anymore; timber is grown on plantations. And travelers are planting trees.

"The best thing people can do," Stephen says, "is to come here to God's garden, to this lost ark, and be inspired to make a difference back home. This forest was saved by ordinary people who decided to do the right thing. Don't go and gawk; go and give back."

COSMOSIS

Ka hinga atu he tetekura—ka ara mai he tetekura.

As one fern frond dies—one is born to take its place.

Next we trundle a little ways north toward a harbor called Hokianga. Traversing this trail is like following a ghost, as we have yet to see a heron, though the incandescent Scot, Ian the guide, assures me this is the way.

At the crest of a small rise, we stop and look down to a body of water that seems to tremble with anticipation. Across the shimmering distance is a long, hazy mouth of a ginger-colored ridge, which for a moment I imagine might tilt down and swallow the whole harbor. My eyes, I realize, are hungry for an end to the immensity of this passage.

European whaling began in earnest at this sublime natural harbor in 1822. But its name harks to an earlier event. After maneuvering his lateen-sail craft around the North Island, naming places as he went, the great Polynesian explorer Kupe settled on the Hokianga Harbor as his temporary home. The words he uttered when he made his eventual trip back home to Hawaiki became the name for the harbor: "Hei konei ra i te puna i te ao marama, ka hoki nei ahau, e kore ano e hokianga-nui mai"— "Farewell, spring of the world of light; I shall not come back here again." The entrance to the harbor is guarded by two headlands named for the *taniwha* (monsters) who accompanied Kupe here. The North Head is Niniwa, and the South Head is Arai-te-Uru. The eleven rivers that feed the Hokianga are the paths their children made.

In Kupe's old age, he pushed his waka back into the ocean and navigated home to Hawaiki to share what he had found, and the rest is Māori history.

Here we meet Koro Carman, the young, energetic manager for Crossings Hokianga, a new Māori-owned tour company that showcases the region, its history, and its stories. Koro was born and raised in the

Hokianga Harbor, where European whaling began in earnest in 1822

Hokianga area, but took off to find his fortune in Auckland. After dipping into the city for a few years, he felt that he was losing his identity—that the city was eroding some of the core concepts that his family had imbued in him since childhood. So he decided to come home and try to make a living celebrating his heritage through tourism.

Koro has us board his new boat, the *Hokianga Express,* at the Opononi wharf. We set lines free from the bollards, and we chug toward the other side of the harbor to a sight few expect to find in New Zealand. The country is well-known for its mountains, glaciers, rain forests, lakes, wild rivers, and rolling green fields, but few would imagine this country is host to some of the most dynamic parabolic sand dunes in the world.

As we approach, I can see the ruffles and flutes of the sands blazing with gold and orange against the hard blue sky. It seems we are in the realm of Antoine de Saint-Exupéry rather than that of Ed Hillary.

We land, and I step out to crawl up a yellow dune, a sensually shaped, honey-colored ridge. With every step, I sink into sand as soft as talcum. It's like wading though first snow.

Once on the plateau, Koro kicks off his shoes and leads me on a stroll. Because he grew up here, at the place where Kupe may have first brought the concept of kaitiakitanga to Aotearoa, I ask whether he has excavated a deeper comprehension than others.

"While I don't completely understand the concept," he says, "I think I can summarize it in one word: *tomorrow.* I'm on a lifelong journey to know kaitiakitanga, but what I do know is that it is about fostering and managing so that we can benefit tomorrow."

If Koro, a Māori born and bred where Kupe landed, thus beginning the radiation of ideas that have lit a millennium, confesses to not fully knowing kaitiakitanga, then I know I can no better fence this concept than I could fence the sky.

It's getting late, and we have to head back to catch a ferry, but I can't resist the call, and so before departing, I back up and then take a run and leap off into the void down a sand dune. I glissade and roll down the yellow sand and come to halt half-buried. I look around. All is motionless as in a picture, caught in a continuous Now, living in the warmth of the late-afternoon sun, with neither past nor future. Then, suddenly, a boil swirls over the quiet surface of the harbor and subsides like a sigh. The *Hokianga Express* is humming. It's time to go.

As we make the crossing back, the pilot tells me that the yellow-bellied flounder is the kaitiaki for this harbor: "It feeds our families." The quip only serves to further confuse, as I would have thought the reverse

The Great Sand Dunes of Hokianga

would be the ethos here: humans saving fish through prudent use. "Anything and everything can be a kaitiaki—and Bob's your uncle," Koro pipes up, and he grins.

We make the short trek across the country, and I turn around to watch the skin of the day cast into the woods. In last light, I revel in the dappled, tree-bowered road that unspools behind us—what finer way to flee a stained and carbonated past? We spend the night on Doubtless Bay, on the Pacific side of this sliver, at the Taipa Bay Resort. Ian and I hover at the bar, munching on wine-colored groundnuts and salt-and-vinegar chips and sipping G&Ts. Ian is wearing a merino sweater so thick it threatens to capsize him. We've traveled a thousand miles together, and I take the moment to ask him again why he thinks New Zealand is such an environmental exemplar.

He considers between digestive sips and then proposes that it is a perfect storm of land, people, and people.

The land is blessed with beauty and abundance on islands perhaps the right size for management. On tiny Easter Island, across the Pacific, the ecosystem collapsed when man cut and burned the trees to a

221

tipping point. North America is so big that what happens on one side isn't readily felt on the other. Size matters. New Zealand is of a volume and range that when things go awry, there is awareness and nimbleness and the chance to self-correct. The law of unintended consequences can be bent back here. Also, its value today is in its wildness and purity—a key reason visitors travel long distances to call—and so the country has a special and compelling incentive to preserve those qualities.

Māori who came here were explorers who had seen many provinces of the Pacific but made Aotearoa home. They fashioned a cosmology that incorporated the lessons seen throughout the world. Living removed and in a place with no ruminants to eat, they learned how to manage resources judiciously. Their closeness to nature, their intimate and intense knowledge of the landscape, led to a worldview that personified all aspects of the environment, recognized everything as sacred, and bound the whole kit and caboodle with indissoluble ties of kinship.

And the Europeans who came here, including Ian's own relatives, were of a stock that inspired a culture of can-do ingenuity. They weren't criminals and lumpenproletariat, as were the early settlers of Australia, or religious refugees, as were many of the first European émigrés to North America. They were stolid, middle-class sorts who volunteered to make the passage to carve out a better life, one disencumbered by narration, sophistic rules, or class. They weren't aristocrats—they were congenitally opposed to unearned pelf. They weren't poor, but they were independent, innovative souls ready to roll up sleeves, figure things out, and make things work. Ian calls this the "number eight fencing wire" mentality, in that anything can be mended or made with the stuff. The early Europeans in New Zealand were pioneers, and they remain so today in so many ways.

The barkeep seems to be listening to our discussion as he wipes a glass, and I ask for his thoughts, but he turns to another customer. So does the waitress. Not everyone fits a paradigm. The little town here is the northernmost settlement in New Zealand with a population of more than one thousand, and it seems to possess a granite indifference to the rest of the country, or the world. But it is the launching point for the final path seeking this cultural Sangreal.

That night as I unpack my bag, I unfold a piece of paper I have carried with me throughout the journey. It is a cream-colored page of notepaper with the blue-ink printed header: "Tom Peirce."

On the page, Tom had hand-copied a meditation from his Aspen school friend, the photographer Chapin Jonathan Wright. On October 13, 1980, renowned mountaineers Rick Ridgeway and Yvon Chouinard, in company with Jonathan Wright on assignment for *National Geographic*, were struggling up the slopes of the little-explored Tibetan mountain Minya Konka when an avalanche swallowed them. Wright, just twenty-eight years old, died. As he did, Ridgeway wrote, "something left him. I saw it." Before Tom died, he gave me this piece of paper, and I have kept it close since:

> *"Mother Nature has let us flounder all night lost in the fog. With the fog she is showing us that life is not always a direct course. You don't always know where you are going. You can only keep fighting on with a smile until the fog lifts and the new light is seen. It might be a different course, but it's life. Thanks for the fog.*

> —Chapin Wright, Summer, 1971

END OF THE LINE

E tae ki Te Rerenga, tahuri mai ki muri, mihi mai i kona
Te riu ki te whenua, e. Tēnei, e te hoa,
A taua kura i waiho i muri i tō tua.
Mā wai hoki rā e pupuri ringa rua?
E here ana mai te taura o te pō hai kukume ki raro rā e.

When you come to the leaping place, turn back and greet
The vale of the land. Friend, these are our treasures
Which you are leaving behind your back.
Who can hold them forever in his hands?
The rope of night binds us and will drag us below.

n the morning I awake in a bit of a fog. I can't find one of my socks; my notebook has gone missing. Somewhere, I've misplaced my certainty.

But I step outside to air so elastic and crystalline it has the same effect on the landscape as glass on a picture. The sunrise of eastern New Zealand is the first the world sees every day, and it rises bright today, as if rewarding good, Māori-inspired thoughts—good, roaring thoughts.

Ian takes the wheel, and we snake our way up the last stingray tail of provenance that is New Zealand toward Cape Te Reinga, the cape of "the leaping place of spirits." Along the way we pass herds of wild horses and the occasional homestead with roofs that seem to have mounded themselves, as if the grass itself had taken definite shape and form. The eaves appear to have parted company from their woodland fellows merely for a moment. Our appearance has disturbed them in movement, and they stand motionless, even though, I imagine, they must have been dancing just seconds ago. This northern nick of land seems touched by some magic wand.

We have to park about a half mile from the white lighthouse that overlooks the cape itself and the spirit tree. William Puckey, a pioneer missionary, was the first European to travel overland to Cape Te Reinga in 1832. He wrote: "The place has a most barren appearance with sea-fowl screaming and the sea roaring and rushing against dismal black rocks. It would suggest to the reflecting mind that it must have been the dreary aspect of the place which led Māori to choose this spot as his hell."

Not wanting to miss the road for the gravel and tar, I walk along a ridge by the pavement through grass that seems to be whispering: "Shhhh; shhhh; shhhh." I walk until I can go no farther because there is no more land. There is a glint along the water. I imagine it is a heron carrying the soul of my friend Tom Peirce. This seems a place for the suspension of disbelief.

I look down a steep cliff to a crooked finger of rock that points to the great Ocean of Kiwa, to a moiling seam where the Tasman Sea shoulders into the Pacific Ocean. There, hanging over the finger's nail, is the pōhutukawa tree that for eight hundred years has resisted the elements, the brutal forces of wind, water, and man. This is the spirit tree to which the white herons fly carrying the souls of Māori. And in the fine, tangled fantasy of its branches, the spirits rest before setting out to return from whence they came.

William Colenso, another early missionary who first printed the New Testament in Māori and was the second European to visit Cape Te Reinga, tried to persuade one of his Māori converts to climb out to the tree and chop it down, but the Māori refused. It is a sacred tree to all Māori, no matter the subsoil of faith.

For a moment the wind dies, and silence is the overwhelming sound. It is a negation so absolute it becomes a positive presence, pressing upon my ears. There is a shiftiness going on, as though the scene before me is being pulled and tugged.

Then, at the irrevocable edge of this world, a Māori woman walks to my side and juts her chin into the wind. She carries a walking stick and turns to it, nods to it, as though it were a friend. Then she turns to me with big lantern eyes. For a long minute, we look at one another, seeking some sort of wordless connection. There is an unseen presence of fellowship in the air. Then she introduces herself. She is Joyce Conrad-Munns, a local guide. She extends her arm to the headland, toward the tree and the water beyond, and speaks to the eschatology of this place. "This is the most important place for Māori. When we pass on, our spirits take the journey to the hilltops near here, then down to Spirits Bay to take a last drink of water, then to the spirit tree, and then to the other world, back to Hawaiki."

The terrestrial mind sees water as the end of relevant life. The great land-based civilizations strove to control water, and such control of water meant people also had to be controlled, to dig the canals, build the weirs, irrigate the crops. Farmers were slaves to water and to authority. Strangers were enemies.

Māori mariners had to be free to meet the ever-changing conditions of water and weather, and while sailing, they were out of authority's reach. Strangers were their friends. When a waka pushed off to head back to its origins, the parted water rejoined unchanged at the stern's trailing edge.

This is the end; there is no more to travel here. And I wonder if I have gained a liminal trace of understanding on this journey—if I have been able to unlearn what I believed I knew and to acknowledge the mystery and stupefying interconnectedness of all things. It seems there is no quantifiable yield. After all this travel, the mind is a sieve of a sort, but left with memories, feelings, images, moments that finally, after time and distance, seem to have begun to arrange themselves as a constellation. What remain uncharted are the unlit pieces of the sky.

What I think I have learned is that Māori believe that all things—rivers, rocks, mountains, the moon, and the mist—have a life force, and that we are all inextricably bound together; we are all fastened by a genealogical web and share in the unfolding frond of the universe. Perhaps that's why this land's concept of caretaking is so worthy of consideration. It is the idea that we are all a part of nature, not separate from it. That simple notion may hold the promise of long tomorrows, and is perhaps a truth for the whole of the world.

The lighthouse at Cape Te Reinga, the cape of "the leaping place of spirits." It overlooks the great Ocean of Kiwa, to a moiling seam where the Tasman Sea shoulders into the Pacific Ocean.

RICHARD BANGS'

Adventures

WITH PURPOSE

AS SEEN
NATIONALLY
ON PUBLIC
TELEVISION!

DISPATCHES FROM
THE FRONT LINES
OF EARTH

To discover more about the adventures of Richard Bangs, read on. "The Quest for the Lord of the Nile" is excerpted from Bangs's recent book *Adventures with Purpose,* from Menasha Ridge Press.

RICHARD BANGS' *Adventures with Purpose*
Dispatches from the Front Lines of Earth

Running wild rivers such as the crocodile-infested Tekaze in Ethiopia, Richard Bangs lived for the adrenaline, for the rush of reveling in the misery of hardship and sidestepping death around every bend. Bangs's classic, *The Lost River,* which recounts first descents in Ethiopia and demands a single-session chair-gripping read, epitomizes the rough-and-ready formative years of Bangs as the explorer's explorer. As Bangs and his compadres survived river after river, a new purpose presented itself, though. Now an eminent and respected conservationist, Web pioneer, ambassador, and explorer, Bangs still travels to exotic and difficult environments, but with a new purpose:

"Over the decades, I have witnessed many special places preserved and lost, and the critical vector in their survival or demise was more often than not the number of visitors who trekked the landscape or floated the river and were touched deeply by their unique beauty and spirit. When such a space became threatened, there was a constituency for whom the place was personal, a collective force ready to lend energy, monies, and time to preservation."

The result of Bangs's philanthropy is now the preservation and promotion of threatened peoples, places, habitats, and animals. *Richard Bangs' Adventures with Purpose* follows Richard from Bosnia to Libya, Panama to the American West, Rwanda to Thailand, all in a search to make sense of disappearing cultures and rivers, to save them by bringing them to life.

In typical Bangs narrative, *Adventures with Purpose* plows to the heart of the matter, painting peoples and places as he weaves among them, creating landscapes that tell their own story.

To order, **visit www.menasharidge.com.**

1

The Quest for the Lord of the Nile

Egypt

> *It is the wisdom of crocodiles, that shed tears*
> *when they would devour.*
> —Francis Bacon, "Of Wisdom for a Man's Self"

The whole business began with an entirely improbable cosmological conjunction, a Nilotic lord in the house of a men's magazine.

In the early 1970s, I was a river guide on the Colorado River through the Grand Canyon, and somehow between trips happened across a copy of *Argosy* magazine, one of those pulp rags that depicted brawny men bare-handedly fighting off large predators, often a grizzly or mountain lion, while scantily clad nymphs swooned in the background. This issue reported on a 1968 rafting expedition down the Blue Nile by a British Army team, a military-style enterprise distinguished for its lack of river-running experience and fatal blunders. One success, though, was with the crocodiles that cruised the eddies. As the unchallenged lords of the river, they would instinctively charge the passing rafts, but as the British hurled baseball-sized rocks back, the crocs would submerge and retreat, perhaps in puzzlement at such counterattack behavior. But the explorers fared less well with the river itself. They flipped boats, sacrificed gear to the boiling currents, and lost one member to drowning. While reading the piece, I realized I knew more than anyone on

231

the British expedition about white-water rafting, and that perhaps I could make a successful descent of the Blue Nile where they had failed.

So I spent the next several months preparing to head to Ethiopia to run the Blue Nile, poring over books describing the many ways I could die attempting such. I learned there was a raft of nasty obstacles that might do damage. The rapids were certainly a given. They were big and dangerous. But then there were hippos, second largest land mammals after elephants, and infamous for turning over boats and snapping occupants in two. The wild buffalo in the region had a reputation for charging unprovoked. I read about puff adders, black mambas, and spitting cobras and about legendary twenty-foot pythons that capsized canoes. And there were a score of documented exotic tropical diseases, from onchocerciasis (river blindness) to elephantiasis; from trypanosomiasis (sleeping sickness) to trichuris (whipworm); from yaws to several fatal forms of malaria. There were the local peoples, some with fierce reputations. The Blue Nile corridor had taken a toll of explorers who had fallen prey to the ruthless *Shifta,* the roaming bands of bandits who ruled the outback. In 1962, a Swiss-French canoeing expedition was attacked in the middle of the night. Four of the party escaped in a single canoe under a hail of gunfire, while the rest lay dead in the campsite.

But the one danger cited over and over was the risk of death by crocodile. The most deadly existing reptile, the man-eating *Crocodylus niloticus* has always been on man's "worst enemies" list. More people are killed and eaten by crocodiles each year in Africa than by all other animals combined. Crocodile hunters, upon cutting open stomachs of their prey, often discovered bracelets and bits of jewelry and human remains. Huge, ravening predators, armed with massive, teeth-studded jaws, strong, unrestrainable, indestructible, and destructive, crocodiles, if given the chance, eat people. It's their nature. The river is their turf, and we would be trespassers. I found myself in cold-sweat nightmares imagining the yellow, chisel-sharp teeth of a giant croc ripping my skin apart. This would be the most awful way to die. But I thought about the alternative—law or graduate school leading to a real job—and facing crocodiles seemed the delightful evil of two lessers.

I read as much as I could find about crocodiles, though I quickly discovered not many people had ever navigated white water in Africa, and of the few who had, and survived, less than a handful had left reliable accounts of their experiences with crocs. I discovered there were two major schools of thought about how to cope while floating a crocodile-infested river: 1) Be as noisy as possible when passing through a crocodile pool to scare them off. 2) Be as silent as possible when passing through a croc-infested area so as not to attract attention. The rationale for the latter method was that since crocodiles have fixed-focused eyesight—they can see things clearly only at one specific distance—a noiseless boat floating past at the proper distance could probably go unnoticed. One expert at the National Zoo even warned not to laugh in a certain manner, as it resembled the sound of an infant croc in trouble, and the noise would alert all larger crocs within hearing distance to rush to the rescue. He demonstrated the laugh, and it sounded eerily like my partner's high-pitched nervous laugh, so I silently vowed to keep topics serious if sharing a raft with John Yost.

Another account was graphically presented in the bestiary *Eyelids of Morning: The Mingled Destinies of Crocodiles and Men,* written by Alistair Graham and photographed by Peter Beard, two researchers who might be considered the anti–Jane Goodall and Dian Fossey in that they studied their charges by hunting them (they shot 500 in the course of a year). In their summary, they recount the saga of a Peace Corps volunteer, Bill Olsen, a recent graduate of Cornell, who decided to take a swim in Ethiopia's Baro River, an eventual tributary to the White Nile, against the advice of locals. He swam to a sandbar on the far side of the muddy river and sat there with his feet on a submerged rock. He was leaning into the current to keep his balance, a rippled vee of water trailing behind him, his arms folded across his chest as he was staring ahead lost in thought. A few minutes later, his friends saw that Bill had vanished without trace or sound. A few more minutes later, a big croc surfaced with a large, white, partially submerged object in its jaws, whose identity was in no doubt. The next morning, a hunter on safari, a Colonel Dow, snuck up on the croc, shot it, and then dragged the carcass to the beach. He cut it open and inside found Bill Olsen's legs, intact from the knees down, still joined at the pelvis. His head, crushed into small chunks, was a barely recognizable mass of hair and flesh. A black and white photo of Bill's twisted, bloody legs dumped in a torn cardboard box drilled into my paraconsciousness, and for days I would shut my eyes and shiver at the image.

In the end, I was not comforted by what I learned in my research—if anything, I was a good deal more afraid.

It was while I was casting about for a name for my expedition that a thin book on the gods of ancient Egypt wrought inspiration. There was Ra, the sun god, but that had been taken by Thor Heyerdahl's recent expedition. There was Hesamut, the hippo goddess depicted in the act of demolishing a crocodile. But *Hesamut Expedition* didn't resonate. One chapter spoke of the crocodile god Sobek, worshipped along the Egyptian Nile. A temple was built to the deity on the island of Kom Ombo between Aswan and Luxor, where mothers of children eaten by crocodiles felt privileged to have provided something for Sobek's delectation. And there were sacrificial pools at a city in the Fayoum Valley called Crocodopolis. The story went that once upon a time, Menes, first king of all the Egyptians, was set upon by his own dogs while out hunting. In his flight he came to the Nile, where lay a large croc baking in the sun. The croc, rapidly sizing up the situation, offered to ferry the desperate king across the river.

With all saurian ceremony, Menes was sculled over to found a city in about 3000 BC that would worship crocodiles, a city that was christened Crocodopolis. Henceforth, it was believed that if Sobek were appeased, he would allow the fragile papyrus boats used to ply the Nile to remain unharmed. About 321 BC, when the army of Perdiccas was crossing the Nile at Memphis, it forgot to pay Sobek homage, and 1,000 soldiers were killed and eaten. Naming my expedition after a deity that would protect boats from sharp-toothed serpents seemed like a good idea to me, so Sobek we became.

The eponym served us well. For the next ten years I made a number of first descents of upper stretches of African rivers, including a section of the Blue Nile that had defeated the British, and though all the rivers were populated by man-eating crocodiles, for the most part they left us alone. Okay, we had a few rafts bitten by crocodiles, but more by hippos, and we suffered no mortification of the flesh. It seemed Sobek was indeed looking kindly upon us, and so in 1983, for our ten-year anniversary, I organized a trip to visit Kom Ombo, the Sobek temple, to pay proper tribute.

It was a quick three-day excursion on a cruise boat, and once at the nearly vacant house of Sobek, where only a few foreign researchers milled about, I drank in the seemingly mystical exhibition of the crocodile god in a gallery of ancient Nilotic scenes. I left an offering of a Sobek catalog, an inscribed Sierra Club cup, and a T-shirt at the base of an engraved depiction of the god. But one thing left me wondering. Throughout the journey we saw not a single live crocodile on the Nile, and when I queried the captain, he said there were none left—they had gone like the pharaohs. In Egypt, he explained, they had all long since vanished, hunted or died out from environmental shifts.

For the next two decades, my colleagues and I continued to run expeditions around the world under the Sobek imprimatur, and for the most part they were successful. But as Sobek saw us through,

I wondered about the source of the mythology and about what had happened to the river dragons, so indestructible, so revered, closest living relatives to the dinosaurs, existing little changed since long before man walked along the Nile, yet now gone.

Then in 2003 I helped organize an expedition that hoped to make the first full descent of the Nile from its Blue Nile source in Ethiopia to the mouth near Alexandria, Egypt. My friend Pasquale Scaturro led the five-month-long voyage, and as I waved good-bye to him on the banks of Lake Tana in the highlands of Ethiopia, he promised to check in every few days on his satellite phone. "Watch out for the crocs. They're always looking for a handout," were my departing words.

Indeed the expedition was charged by several large crocodiles as it made its way down off the Abyssinian plateau and into Sudan. A kayak paddle was chomped at one point. But the real surprise was when Pasquale passed into Lake Nasser in Upper Egypt. He called and reported, "You wouldn't believe the size of the crocodiles here. They're monsters!" I was surprised and in some strange way delighted with that news. I had thought crocodiles were gone from Egypt, but they were, according to Pasquale, coming back, in a big way.

So it was I crafted a confection, to travel to Egypt and follow the Nile upstream from Alexandria to Upper Egypt and Lake Nasser to inquire a little into the crocodiles in myth and history, and know why they disappeared and how they might be returning, a quest for the Lord of the Nile. I owed a lot to Sobek and wanted to see if I might mine some understanding and perhaps find a way to give back.

The Eastern Harbor of Alexandria curves like a scimitar at the edge of the Nile Delta. It was here that crocodiles in great numbers lingered at the stitch of fresh water and salt water, a seam rich with nutrients and fish. During the annual flood, some were swept seaward and found their ways to shores as distant as the Aegean and the Levantine Coast.

In the time of the Ptolemys, this port was the center of learning of the civilized world, and texts and manuscripts were brought to its library from everywhere writing existed. But during the time of Julius Caesar, the library was burned, and the city fell into decline.

The ancient library has been replaced by a new one, the Bibliotheca Alexandrina, spearheaded by UNESCO and completed in 2002.

Crossing the wide boulevard of the Corniche, I head into the tilted, circular building that with a squint looks like a rising sun. I find my way across the cantilevered study halls to one of the hundreds of computer terminals and there begin to scroll through the titles, assuming that if there is a repository of information on the reptiles of the Nile, and Sobek, it would be here.

After I pore over tomes, a possible explanation for one of the riddles of the Nile begins to emerge. It was the crocodile, in a fashion, that was responsible for the pyramids and the great tombs of Egypt.

The ancient Egyptians watched helpless each summer as the life-giving Nile receded and left their fields barren. Then come September, under clear blue skies, the river would run in spate, bringing swarms of crocodiles and the rich soil and nutrients that would replenish the black and dead soil. It was a mystery from where the crocodiles and the new soil came, and why, but the Egyptians looked on as lifeless land was reborn and crocodile eggs were laid with the season.

Just as the sun died and was reborn each day, so the soil was resurrected along the Nile each year as the crocodiles came. Crocodile eggs hatched and created life out of nothing. These annuities, it might be conjectured, gave the Egyptians the idea that the crocodile was the agent for this rebirth, giving them reason to believe they too could restart life after death.

So Sobek became a god of fertility and rebirth, and Egyptians inferred that if Sobek could give the land a new life, then he could do the same for humans. Accordingly, the pharaohs endorsed the concept of an afterlife and believed they could bring possessions with them. So they built enormous tombs, filled them with their effects, and had themselves mummified in preparation for the journey. Perhaps as guides to the afterlife, crocodiles were also embalmed in sarcophagi in these tombs, placed alongside canopic jars filled with vital organs necessary for the hereafter.

If this theory is true, I am not the only one who owes a debt to Sobek. So does everyone who has ever admired the pyramids, or the tombs of the Valley of the Kings as well, monumental aesthetic gifts that have endured for millennia.

Of no surprise, this library carries the Egyptian Book of the Dead, the cheat sheet to the afterlife for dynastic Egyptians, rich with references to Sobek. In one passage the crocodile god speaks:

"I am the owner of seed who takes women from their husbands whenever he wishes, according to his desire. I am Sobek, who carries off by violence."

A key description in chapter 125 of the Book of the Dead is that of the weighing of the heart, a precursor to the Christian concept of the Last Judgment. The heart of the newly dead was placed on one side of a scale. On the other side was a feather from the goddess Maat, who represented order and justice. Looming nearby was the hell mouth of a crocodile-headed monster.

If the scale balanced, the god of the underworld, Osiris, would lead the deceased to reanimation in the next world. If unbalanced, the heart was tossed to the crocodile-headed monster and devoured.

Sobek as a spirited demiurge was associated with death, but also sex. In the Pyramid Text (spell 510), Sobek's lusty stealth and sexual potency are described, wherein the king changes into a crocodile before robbing husbands of their wives. Another passage speaks to Sobek's contravening powers: women would use the dung of crocodiles as contraceptives.

Still other texts suggest it is a stroke of good fortune to be gobbled by a crocodile. And so it is that the relationship with the Nile crocodile is a conflicted one; the croc was feared and worshipped, seen as an instrument of death, fertility, regeneration, and channel to the next world.

The brilliance of the ancient imaginings of Sobek is that their current of moral energy ran both ways, just as the Nile for navigation. Creator, destroyer; good, evil; a god, the devil. Like its amphibious nature, between land and water, the god evoked ambiguity, a place between and of, a duality in motion, ultimately a spiritual device that covered all bases.

After scouring the library, I can find no reference to crocodiles returning to the Nile, so I set out upstream to see if I can find the lost beast and make some sort of approbation.

From Alexandria I wind up the estuarine Nile to Cairo, where the river turns like some grave thought threading a dream. Here the Nile grinds and clanks with an incessant bass note at the frame of the delta, polluted, noisy, demanding. If a crocodile wanted to live in the noxious waters here today, it couldn't. Past sand-colored mosques and beneath the mullioned windows, I comb the streets looking for any evidence of a crocodile, but come up with nothing, save a popular extract of crocodile, a philter ointment whose label says, "For you and your happiness." Finally, I step down an alley into the heart of the Khan al-Khalili bazaar, a frantic mélange of old smells and snaking Arabic sounds.

I encounter a man in a beaded robe who tells me I can find a crocodile at El-Fishawi Café and offers to guide me there. I imagine a crocodile, traded like a slave from the south, in some tub in the back, and if so, I know I will want to negotiate to set it free. But as I step into the hazy, hookah-filled cafe and ask where I might find this wayward animal, a waiter nods to a candy-striped arched doorway. As I lift eyes above the archway, I spy a five-foot crocodile stuffed and nailed as though in a Victorian trophy room. He is the closest thing to an intact crocodile I will find in Cairo.

Deeper in the bazaar, among the pricelessly bad tourist baubles, I ask the merchants if they have any crocodiles to sell. Ever since Herodotus, Egyptians have welcomed foreigners with an admixture of banter, hearty browbeating, effusiveness, and the sort of insincere familiarity associated with people trying to become intimate enough to pick a pocket. So when one man offers to take me up the narrow stairs to his shop, I proceed with caution. There he sits me down and offers me tea. In the furbe-lows and folderol of the chat between the first cup and the second he shows me several interpretations of crocodiles in soapstone and wood, but nothing real. Then into the second cup he asks me to wait and disappears down the stairs. A few minutes later, he emerges with the gnarled, rolled skin of a seven-foot crocodile. His price is $2,000, and I pass, declining to bargain. He won't tell me where he got it, or any details. It was likely poached, and just negotiating could encourage the illegal trade. So I instead bid on a beautiful, handmade Egyptian-cotton abaya. I manage to get him down to half his initial price and feel pretty good with the deal until the next day when I eye the same robe in the hotel window for another half off the price.

Before I arrived in Egypt, there was a flurry of e-mail exchanges with Eva Dadrian, a Cairo-based reporter for the BBC. I had asked if she could track down any experts on croco-diles, and she found but one: Dr. Sherif Baha El Din, an environ-mental consultant and herpetologist who has been surveying the scaly wildlife of Lake Nasser.

In his cluttered Cairo apartment, ornamented equally with toddler toys and renditions of reptiles, I ask Dr. El Din what hap-pened to the crocodiles of the Nile.

"A combination of things. Certainly human population pressure over the centuries . . . increasing numbers of people competing with wildlife for the river, and winning." Dr. El Din continues to elaborate, citing the first Aswan Dam, finished in 1902, as a primary culprit. It effectively blocked the annual floods, which washed down new populations of crocodiles each year. Now crocodiles are locked upstream.

But it is the lust for crocodile leather that really wiped out the crocodiles in the twentieth century, a madness for handbags, shoes, belts, and other pelt accessories. By the 1950s, professional hunters from all over the world were coming to Egypt to bag crocodiles, not only for their valuable skins, but also for their meat, a delicacy to some gourmands, and their fat, used as a curative for rheumatic diseases. By the early 1980s, the crocodiles of the Egyptian Nile were all gone. That coincided with my 1983 Sobek anniversary trip.

"When did they start to return?"

"In the mid-1980s, Egypt passed a ban on hunting crocodiles, in the wake of CITES [the Convention on International Trade of Endangered Species of Wild Fauna and Flora] putting Nile crocodiles on the list of endangered species. Since then, crocodiles have started to reappear on Lake Nasser, but not yet in the main Nile. The fishermen hate the crocodiles, who compete for their fish, get caught in and cut their nets, and sometimes attack and eat them, so they continue to kill the crocodiles when the government isn't looking. And there is still a lot of poaching and smuggling going on, even professional hunting safaris for well-heeled foreigners."

"If they are such deadly menaces, why not just hunt them to extinction?"

Dr. El Din argues that crocodiles are an integral part of our natural heritage and ecosystem, a link in the chain of global diversity, and have as much right to share space on the planet as any other creature. They were in fact here millions of years before people and could claim first rights. They were in a fashion the first Egyptians. Through the rise and fall of empires, from the ancient pharaohs to the Ptolemys, through the epochs of the Greeks, Romans, Persians, Arabs, Ottomans, French, and English, only the crocodiles stayed the same, until recently.

But I wonder how the fishermen can ever be convinced? The returning crocodiles affect their livelihood, their well-being.

"Ecotourism" is Dr. El Din's answer. He thinks a viable economic alternative to fishing would be making the wild crocodiles a tourist attraction, just as the gazetted paradises of sub-Saharan Africa have done with lions, Australia's Great Barrier Reef has done with sharks, and the Canadian outpost of Churchill has done with polar bears. "Crocodiles are a very valuable resource and can be a significant tourist attraction. People want to see wild crocodiles in the sun."

Dr. El Din then describes how he has confiscated crocodiles from traders in the Aswan area and liberated them back to the Nile. He concludes by advising, "If in your travels you find a captured crocodile, set it free, if you can. Set an example. It could be a small gesture that saves a life, sends a message, and makes a difference. And the crocodile will then pray for you."

On the outskirts of Cairo is Giza, where I hire a camel and clop to see the great pyramids in the soft coral flush of dawn. Built some 4,500 years ago as way stations to the afterlife, they are the lineaments of gratified desire. No matter how many images one's seen of the pyramids, when in their presence the mind is slendered by awe. If there is architecture of happiness, it is the pyramids, ancient elevators to a higher life.

I continue then south to Saqqara, through a land that looks like the scrapped hide of a camel, bits of hair still tufted to its tawny back. Saqqara is a vast, ancient burial ground featuring the world's oldest standing step pyramid.

While Memphis was the capital of ancient Egypt, Saqqara served as its graveyard. It remained an important complex for burials and cult ceremonies for more than 3,000 years, well into Ptolemaic and Roman times. It is here I hook up with Dr. Zahi Hawass, head of the Supreme Council of Antiquities, and a man temperamentally disinclined to keep any achievement quiet. Hawass wears brushed jeans, a pressed denim shirt, and his signature Indiana

Jones hat, one he tells me is about to be licensed under his brand by a Chicago haberdashery. His famous enthusiasm bubbles when I ask him about Sobek.

"Sobek . . . that is so interesting. Nobody studies Sobek, but he was an important god. In fact, I just made two discoveries. Let me show you."

I follow Dr. Hawass's hat down into a dig in progress, where workers are sifting through a mud-brick tomb that dates back 4,200 years, to the start of the Fifth Dynasty in the Old Kingdom. Grave robbers unearthed this tomb a few months previous, making it the newest major archaeological discovery in Egypt.

Dr. Hawass uncorks his theory that three royal dentists are interred in these tombs, and points out hieroglyphs of an eye over a tooth, the symbol of the men who tended teeth.

Then he says the tomb is marked with a curse and points to a depiction of a crocodile with a beautifully curved tail, one of the oldest illustrations ever discovered of a crocodile: "The dentist put an inscription to say: 'Anyone who enters my tomb will be eaten by the teeth of Sobek.'"

"What about you?" I ask Dr. Hawass.

"Well, the thieves went to jail. As for me . . ." And he stretches a smile like a hammock, hanging out his belief in his own immunity.

Dr. Hawass then signals a couple of his workers, who carry down into the excavation site what looks like a large loaf of bread wrapped in a linen bandage. It is a crocodile mummy found in the house of an antiquities dealer near Giza recently. "The crocodile was the god of rebirth, and in the ancient Egyptian quest for immortality, bringing Sobek with you secured a safe passage to the afterworld."

Dr. Hawass's dig is off in an isolated, anhydrous patch, but just off the road is the famous tomb of Mereruka, a popular tourist walk-through. I join the throngs and file through the labyrinthine chambers and catacombs, past storyboards of a hippopotamus hunt, fowling in the marshes, dwarfs making jewelry, scenes of fishing, gardening, and farming, an ancient catalog of harmonic balance that reverses the telescope from today's hardships and irredentism.

There are enough plot elements in these halls to fill a periodic table. As I sweep my flashlight about, I keep looking for the long-nosed image, and there at last it is, in a fight scene in which a hippo is breaking the back of a crocodile, a not uncommon eschatological picture. Without death, of course, there can be no resurrection. In the Egyptian Book of the Dead, the deceased pass through a series of gates guarded by crocodiles. The correct answer to a riddle opens the gate and leads the way to the everworld.

From Saqqara, I trundle down into the Fayoum Valley, a depression some fifty miles southwest of Cairo and well below sea level, a place burly with old heat. It was here the greatest worship of Nile crocodiles took place, in a city founded by Menes of the First Dynasty and named Crocodopolis. The rulers under the Ptolemys took Sobek to a new level, claiming he was the father of Zeus in the Greek pantheon.

At a withering resort on the edge of Lake Qarun, we sip mint tea and look out at brightly painted fishing boats. Although you would not know from the graciousness and hospitality, this is an oasis where Muslim fundamentalism runs deep into the subsoil, and recent terrorist acts were supposedly plotted along these shores. This valley has long been a fertile bed for severe ideas.

Just up a tor above Lake Qarun, under a glare so fierce it roasts the eyes, I meet Dutch-born archaeologist Dr. Willeke Wendrich, associate professor at UCLA, who is overseeing a dig at Karanis in the heart of Crocodopolis. Karanis was the first Greco-Roman site excavated in Egypt, starting in 1895, and more than 100,000 archaeological objects have been recovered to date.

As she sweeps her hand along the dusty ruins, she says, "This area was once infested with crocodiles." She explains that not only did the annual deluge wash in hordes of crocodiles, but also when the waters retreated the crocodiles remained, lurking in puddles, pools, and fields, creating a constant threat. In an attempt to control this powerful and highly evocative beast, the people deified the crocodile, building at least two large pedestal temples to Sobek here to pay homage, often through sacrifices on altars.

We are standing in one, the limestone-based Southern Temple, in the central temenos of which rests a large stone altar, where one can only imagine what took place. Alongside is a concealed opening where, some speculate, priests hid and gave oracles, pretending they were Sobek, a sort of *Wizard of Oz* behind-the-curtain spectacle. Anatomizing a temple, though, like interpreting a hieroglyph, risks missing the unanalyzable spirit of the thing, its beautiful and hazardous play in a time we can never know.

On each side of the altar are ovenlike compartments, niches where sacred crocodiles, mummified with natron, were placed on biers. Out in the courtyard is what looks like a pool, and we know from Herodotus and other travel writers of the day that crocodiles were kept in pools and bedecked with golden necklaces and bracelets, glass earrings and pendants and other jewels, and hand-fed grain, meat, and wine mixed with milk and honey. It was an early form of ecotourism, a Roman holiday, so to speak, in that pilgrims from the other side of the Mediterranean came here for a chance to see a croc up close, and they paid for the privilege.

The temple seems to have been abandoned around the middle of the third century AD, about the time faith in Sobek as a god and savior waned, coinciding with one of the intervallic droughts. The droughts seemed to prove not only the pharaoh's vulnerability, but also the fact that no matter what homage was paid to Sobek, he didn't, or couldn't, bring the all-important flood sometimes.

From Fayoum, I drive back to the Nile proper and sail up the waters early texts cite as the sweat of Sobek, toward old Thebes, Luxor, and the Valley of the Kings. The middle section of the Nile is unhurt by wonder, defined by the sweat of the working class, full of factories, pylons, roofless brick dwellings, and mud huts adorned with satellite dishes.

Passing to Upper Egypt, the river again spills its romance, sighing around a bend shaped like a crocodile tail. At the water's edge is a colony of reeds, glistening and dancing as the current strolls the margins, stroking stems with fluid fingers. And there is a feast of birds—weavers, kingfishers, darters, cranes, herons, and of course, Egyptian geese flying in wedges around our craft.

Stepping into the Valley of the Kings at dawn, it is quiet and cool, as though the whole of the Nile Valley is holding its breath. The alabaster shops are closed; no urchins tug at the cuffs. Within the shafts of sunlight, platelets of dust move as if in obedience to the rhythms of ancient, silent slaves carrying their burdens.

But then the first of the tourist buses arrives, and then the next, and next, and on and on.

No summer theme-park crunch can describe the experience at the Valley of the Kings: waves and waves of tourists, like warriors from Middle-earth, pour into the tombs, and just when it seems there may be an ending to the crowds, another wave rolls in, tourists from every faucet of the world. Amid this valley of babble I manage to squeeze into a couple of tombs, and there, among many tales from the crypt, I find some vivid renditions of Sobek, seemingly guarding the entrance, open jaws facing outward. Sobek was seen as a powerful protector of tombs from not only raiders but also the deceased in the next life, just as the crocodile seemed to protect the fields. The crocodiles swept throughout the fields during the flood, keeping grass eaters such as hippos and livestock at bay.

In one tomb there is a crypt holding the mummy of a long-tailed crocodile. In another there are neat rows of drawings of the clawed beast in dramatic, frangible moments, scenes of life that reach across the centuries and move today's viewer because the backdrops seem in many ways so contemporary. We may worship different gods, but we still eat, drink, dance, hold hands, and hope there is an afterlife.

The pharaohs gave Sobek his due, but the veneration continues today, in different forms. From the cruise-ship dock I hire a high-masted felucca, one with a sail promoting a local beer, to take me a couple of miles to Crocodile Island, where the worship is alive and well at the Mövenpick Luxor Resort. Everything is croc-themed, from the tiered garden walls decorated with an infinity of crocodiles to "Sobek Hall," the conference center, to the swampy pool on the grounds that houses a lone live crocodile to the famous Crocodile Bar, where under a tapestry of a hungry croc with mouth agape I pay my homage and order a weapons-grade fruffy fruit drink and toast the mighty god.

Refreshed, I chuff upriver to the greatest temple to Sobek ever built. Six hundred miles south of Alexandria, the Ptolemaic ruin of Kom Ombo stands on a bend of the river, looking almost painterly upon approach, like the watercolors of nineteenth-century Nile explorations. While now a jut of mainland, the site was once an island for much of the year with the Nile's high water. Because it could be defended, it was also a main trading center for gold, spices, even elephants moving from Nubia in the south to the ports of the Mediterranean in the north. But while Egyptians here had protection from human invaders, their boats were often seized by crocodiles, and so they built a temple to Sobek in hopes he might look kindly upon their passages. In one surviving text, a man instructs his son to study so as to avoid menial jobs such as that of the washerman who "launders at the riverbank in the vicinity of the crocodile" or the fisherman "who is at his work in a river infested with crocodiles."

In a small shrine within the temple, mummified crocodiles from a nearby sacred animal cemetery are on display, their great scutes and withered limbs the color of antique wood. A hundred years ago, a workman excavating tombs flung aside a mummified crocodile, and it burst open. Papyrus with fragments of lost works from Sophocles, Homer, and Euripides spilled from the belly of the beast.

Now the cruise ships debouch tourists, thousands upon thousands who hungrily snap images of Sobek with their digital cameras and cell phones as they are processed in crocodile files through the sandstone arches, some not knowing where they are. I overhear one tourist ask a local guide, "Is this the Parthenon?" Wandering about myself, I feel as though I've returned to an old play but am no longer playing the same part, recast now as the audience. Sobek seemed almost a sacred secret to me more than two decades ago. Now he is an amusement park ride in a culture of massclusivity.

From Kom Ombo, I unravel the Nile once more, sailing south, the wind at my back, companioned by time and the river flowing. I purl past blistering cliffs and folding pages of orange sand, past feluccas puffing by islands, up a river that dreams along like a giant sleeping. The parted water rejoins unchanged at my stern's trailing edge, but the still shore whispers of a wilder time. Once these banks were crawling with crocodiles.

I arrive at last at the First Cataract, the site of the two Aswan dams. The second, the 364-foot-tall High Dam, was completed in 1970. Without the Nile, the desert would swallow Egypt like a pill. But the dams have tamed the desert. The crocodile was for millennia the most formidable creature in Egypt. But the dams have conquered the beast.

The Nile backs up for almost 300 miles now in one of the largest man-made lakes in the world, some 162 billion cubic yards of water in storage. The rising lake drowned towns and temples, buried significant archaeological sites, and dislocated some 90,000 Nubians, one of the largest human rights abuses in the history of dam building.

The still water behind the dam has become a brew-pot for schistosomiasis, a deadly disease transmitted by infected snails. The mineral-rich silt deposits from the yearly floods, which made the Nile floodplain fertile, are now held behind the dam, and the downstream water is becoming increasingly saline. Where there were once twenty-four kinds of fish, only twelve remain. The mongoose and otter have gone the way of the crocodile. Fishing throughout the whole of the Mediterranean has declined without the nutrients that used to flow freely into the delta.

Then there are the global repercussions. There is an accelerating erosion of coastlines (due to lack of sand, once delivered by the Nile) all along the eastern Mediterranean. And the whole Mediterranean Sea has seen an increase in salinity, with altered current quality traced hundreds of miles into the Atlantic. Some scientists predict the dam's effect on this outflow may contribute to the next ice age, a cog in an engine chugging toward global weather change.

I cross the engineering feat of the High Dam, commemorated by a jagged concrete lotus poking harsh petals to the sky, proclaiming friendship to the Soviet builders of the dam. The zenith of that god, the Communist one, has also passed.

Security here is extreme, as the dam is perhaps the most prominent terrorist target in Africa, yet after much negotiation, and some baksheesh, I am able to make it to the shores of Lake Nasser behind the dam, where I meet a group of fishermen. They have fished these waters all their lives, as did their fathers and their fathers' fathers. I ask about crocodiles in the lake, and they say they are indeed coming back, and in such numbers and size they are more than a nuisance. They find no spiritual utility, no sentiment or fancy with the crocodiles. The crocs' presence makes their traditional fishing waters a stew of anxiety. A colleague was pulled into the water during the last Ramadan and chomped to death. One fisherman shows me his hand, which is missing a thumb, torn off by a crocodile snagged in his night net. Although it's illegal, they sometimes kill the larger crocodiles, and smaller ones they sell to Nubians as tourist attractions. I ask them about tourism as an alternative to their own livelihoods, and they just give me a blank stare. Remote from the temples of preservation, they can't imagine doing anything other than what they do and what their families have always done.

That night I head to the pulsing potamic souq, more unruly and wanton than the counterpart in Cairo, where the shop-keepers hustle visitors like dice, shaking and prodding until the right answer rolls. Through a foyer done in Egyptian porphyry there is a shop called Che Guevara, kept by a smartly dressed young Nubian named Moustafa Abd El Kader. He waves me in and attempts to vend cobra, cheetah, and crocodile goods: belts, handbags, wallets, even the recombinant art form of a dagger with a baby crocodile claw handle. Flush with unearned familiar-ity, he describes the quality and puts a flame to a belt to prove it's not plastic. He lets me fondle a purse, sturdy and sensual, and volunteers that he personally hunts for the goods in his shop, and offers he could broker a live crocodile by tomorrow.

I ask him about ecotourism as a substitute for killing the crocs, and he dismisses the concept with a wave. He holds up a belt and says there is just too much money in the crocodile trade, and business is booming; tourism will never compete. ·

The next day I find myself at a Nubian village as Disney might have imagined it. It consists of a series of families moved just downstream of the dam as Lake Nasser filled. They have recast their lives as tourist attractions, and their homes are filled with baubles and kitsch to hawk to the crucible of tourists who pass through each day.

Nailed above the doorstep to one home is a five-foot croco-dile stuffed with straw, his teeth in a death grip around the neck of cormorant. Not long ago, crocodiles were hung thusly as tal-ismans to protect inhabitants from the evil eye, but now they are simply tourist draws.

In a neighbor's home I meet Ahmed, a watery-eyed man in a white turban who shows me a glass cage with a bamboo lattice top stuffed with adolescent crocodiles, folded and bent to fit into the cramped space. If crocodiles are relics and symbols of the savagery we mean to rise above, these little reptiles defy that notion, their eyes fogged with discomfort and helplessness, their eyelids of mourning. Ahmed pokes one with a stick, and back it sends a disconsolate hiss. These crocodiles, smuggled from the lake, are tourist magnets, until they become too big, when they are killed for their leather and offered to brokers and the shops in the bazaar. This is not the ecotourism that Dr. El Din imagined.

So I ask what it would take to liberate one of the crocodiles. Ahmed says it is expensive and difficult to poach these "protected" creatures and offers to allow the release for $1,000. I counter with $500, and with little hesitation he agrees. So he chooses one of the crocodiles, a relatively docile one about three and a half feet in length, and hands him to me as he fetches a cardboard Aquafina box. I clutch the little monster with one hand tight around his bulging neck, the other gripped at his pitted tail, his power coursing up my arms. Then he thrashes his body about, driving his nose into my chest like a mallet to a tent peg, and I wrestle in terror, not knowing if he is attempting to attack or flee. He snaps his sixty-four sharp teeth and lashes his tail for a few awful seconds, but then calms, as though in trust, or waiting. I quickly drop him into the box, which I recognize in a flash as the same size and shape as the one in which Bill Olsen's legs were dumped along the Baro River. Ahmed quickly shuts the lid. Then to a remote edge of the lake we drive, to a spot safe from the blessings of civilization.

The shoreline has a pale, sun-sucked color, shadowless and uniform. We set the box on the coarse sand, pull back the cardboard, and lift out the lucky crocodile, his cold scales like the heads of small nails. Gently we place him on the ground, careful to avoid a snap, and on the count of three release him. He seems uncertain. He skitters forth a bit, but then stalls a few feet from the water. The lake is making small lapping sounds, like a giant taking sips from a mug.

I give the little croc a boost with my boot, and he sculls along the hot sand, makes a little leap into the water, and begins to propel away to freedom. Watching his little ripple deliquesce, it's hard to appreciate the antipathy for crocodiles, the human urge to rid the world of such life, though I well know this fellow would easily bite the hand that frees him, and in a few years' time would hesitate not a lick to swallow me whole. Yet in some way we must know there is a complexity, indeterminacy, and interconnectedness to all living things, and that it is a mistaken belief that humans are apart from nature. We have for millennia sought dominion over all wildlife, but by eliminating a natural torment, altering a balance that has endured since the morning of humankind, as did the dams with the Nile, there are results unforeseen, consequences that could raze that which was meant to be safeguarded in the first place. Once you mess with equilibrium, as when opening an Egyptian tomb, the essence is liable to crumble, and the world may well turn out to be a more dangerous place for all our efforts to tame it.

Ahmed offers a gap-toothed smile, the wrinkles of his face cracking like a windscreen hit by a stone. He lifts his hand and waves to the departing crocodile, who melts away into the green water. The sublime question is his postdeliverance fate. He may be recaptured and end up in another cage. He may be hunted. He may hunt a fisherman or more. He may become the magic glass into which our fears pour and out of which mythic beasts step. Or he may simply live a long and prosperous life, becoming once again a reason for tourists to come to Egypt, to be awed once more by the Lord of the Nile.

Page references followed by *p* indicate photographs.

Adams, Ruth, 68
Adventure Central, vii
AdventureLink, vii
Adventures with Purpose (documentary), vii
Air New Zealand, 195–99
Akyeampong, Emmanuel, 1
All Blacks (New Zealand national rugby team),
    85–86
Anupam Gupta, vii
Aotearoa (land of the long white cloud).
    See also New Zealand, viii, 36
Archdale, David, 130
Archdale, Sara, 130
Aristotle, 104
ATTA (Adventure Travel Trade Association), vii
Aubrey, Paul, vi, 31, 32

Bangs, Richard, viii, ix, 4*p*, 8*p*, 33*p*, 63*p*, 176*p*
Bangs, Walker T., v, 170, 172, 175, 176*p*
Banks, Joseph, 125
Barrett, John, v, 156, 159–61, 163
Bauer, Karel, vii
Baxter, Andrew, 107
Bay of Islands, 209–16*p*
Beck, Kim, vii
Bellbirds, 168
Benedict XVI, Pope, 35
Billy the Kid (Jack Russell terrier), v, 170
Birdlife
    bellbirds, 168
    declining population of kiwi, 163–65*p*
    extinction of species of, 33, 125
    found on Kapiti Island, 156–61
    Māori myths on, 167, 226
    moa (flightless bird), 33
Blake, William, 168
Blythe, John, v, 170

Boyd massacre (1809), 190–92
Brooklyn Wind Turbine, 137–39
Brown, Alister, v, 141–44
Bruce, Wally "The Wonderman," 132
Brunner, Thomas, 50
Buck, Sir Peter, 161
Burra, Noriko, vi
Busby, Hekenukumai "Hector," vii

Callaghan, Kevin, vii
Cape Te Reinga, 225–28*p*
Carbon emissions, 115–16
Carman, Koro, vi, 218–21
Car Parts Trail, 135–37
Cassin, Greg, 197
Charles, Prince, 209
Chouinard, Yvon, 223
Clarke, Arthur C., 49
Clark, Helen, v, 19, 112, 195, 203
Clark, Minnie, v
Climate change, 115–16
Coburn, Marie, vi, 51
Cohen, Howard, vii
Colenso, William, 226
Collins, Jim, 197
Colorado River
    author on leading tours on, 47–48
    environmental policies governing, 17
    Kiwi expedition along the, 14–15
Conrad-Munns, Joyce, vi, 226–27
Conroy, Patty, vii
Conservation. *See also* Environment;
    Kaitiakitanga
    distinguishing kaitiakitanga from, 75–76
    early Māori lack of, 14, 33, 213, 216
    eco-lodges built in keeping with, 31*p*, 41
    issues facing modern New Zealand, 199–201

Conservation. *(continued)*
    propellerless river craft as, 47*p*
    rāhui (Māori management technique)
        approach to, 105
    Wanaka Homestead adherence to principles
        of, 40–44
Conservation policies
    development of modern, 76
    DOC (New Zealand's Department of
        Conservation) approach to, 105, 107,
        138
    managing paua (abalone), 141–42
    Marine Mammals Protection Act (1978)
        on, 93
    protecting dolphins, whales, and fish re
        sources, 102–07
    sustainability goals of, 203–07
Cook, James, 44, 50, 125, 127, 130, 180, 189
Cook, Tina, vi
Creation story myth, 34
Crozet, Julien, 127–28
Culhane, Michael, vii
Cyclone Eline (2000), 2

Darwin, Charles, 117, 210
Davos World Economic Summit, 204
Deforestation. *See also* Forests
    Easter Island, 221–22
    of kauri forests, 213, 216
DOC (New Zealand's Department of
        Conservation), 105, 107, 138
Dods, Jude, vii
Dolphins, 93–94*p*, 98, 104*p*–07
Ducker, Lucinda, vi
D'Urville, Dumont, 50

Easter Island, 221
Eco-lodges, 31*p*, 41
Ekehu (Māori guide), 50–51

Emerald Terrace, 188
Energy resources
    Brooklyn Wind Turbine, 137–39
    changing approach by New Zealand to, 135
Environment. *See also* Conservation;
        Kaitiakitanga
    climate change/global warming and the,
        115–16
    extinction of species, 33, 125
    greenhouse gases and, 115–16, 180, 200–201
    John Panoho on Māori beliefs about the, 23–24
    two opposing creeds regarding man and, 173
    witnessing global devastation of, 2–5
Ewing, Alex, v, 29
Extinction of species, 33, 125

FART (Fight Against Ridiculous Taxes), 180
Federated Farmers of New Zealand, 180
Fischer, Scott, 177, 178
Fishing industry
    paua (abalone) conservation and, 141–42
    policies protecting dolphins, whales, and
        fish resources, 102–07
Flax, 167–68
The Flying Fox, 170, 171
Forests. *See also* Deforestation
    kauri tree, 213–16
    pōhutukawa tree (Cape Te Reinga
        spirit tree), 226
Franz Josef Glacier, 53–55*p*
Franz Josef Glacier Country Retreat, 51, 53–55
Fresne, Joseph Marion du, 127
Funkhouser, Chris, vii
Fyffe, George, 110
Fyffe, Robert, 93
Fyffe View Ranch, 120–22, 123*p*
Gardiner, Dale, 14*p*, 16–17
Gibson, Craig, vii
Gibson, Pip, vii

Gibson, Susan, vi
Gidney, Nelsa, vii
Gill, Steve, vi, 116, 117–18
Givens, John, vii
Givens, Sara, vii
Global Volunteer Network ("Ngā Kaitiaki"),
    149, 152
Global warming, 115–16
Gold, Neroli, vi
Gore, Al, 115
Gray, W., 81
Green Globe, 40, 111
Greenhouse gases, 115–16, 180, 200–201
Haast, Johann Franz Julius von, 46
Haitana, Baldy, v
haka (Māori war dance), 161–62
Hall, Rob, 177–78
Hamilton, Bill, v, 145–46
Hamilton, Jon, vi, 14–15
Hamilton, Sir William, 14, 47
hāngi (meal cooked in the earth), 145
Harnish, Grant, v
Hay bundles, 82*p*
Heaphy, Charles, 50–51
Heays, Kevin, vi, 110–12, 113, 120
Hector, Sir James, 103–04
Heisenberg uncertainty principle, 178
Helicopter tours, 31–32
Hellebrekers, Tess, vi
Helms, Russell, vii
Henderson, Bart, vi, 14
The Heritage (hotel), 194–95
High Country Passage, 4
Hikurangi Trench, 98
Hillary, Sir Edmund
    acknowledgment given to, v
    ecumenical application of kaitiakitanga
      by, 57–71
    pioneering ascents of, 15, 57, 58*p*

    on the spirit of past great men, 56
    Tom Peirce on his first meeting with, 194
Hill, Jim, v, 183–87
Hinenuitepo (goddess of night and death),
    88–89
Hock, Dee, 123
Hokianga Express, 219, 220
Hokianga Harbor, 218–21
Hokianga sand dunes, 221*p*
Hooker Glacier (Mount Cook), 62–63*p*, 68–70
Hotel d'Urville, 133
Hubber, Laura, vii
Hulme, Keri, 73
Husbandry industry, 180, 201

Indrakusuma, Halim, 3–4
Innovative Waste Kaikoura, 116

Jackson, Peter, 131
Jarvis, Lyn, 131
Jarvis, Roger, 131
Johnck, Didrik, vii

K2 (Pakistan), 63–64
Kahu, Kim, 84
Kaikoura (South Island)
    early whaling industry in, 93
    environmental efforts begun by, 110–13
    Trees for Travellers program of, 116–18
    visiting Fyffe View Ranch before leaving,
      120–22
    whale-watching tours from, 99–100
Kain, Lindsay, vi, 46–47
Kai (restaurant), 145–46
Kaitiaki Adventures, 8, 10
Kaitiaki (human agent), 77
Kaitiakitanga. *See also* Conservation;
    Environment; Māori culture
chaordic explanation of, 123

Kaitiakitanga. *(continued)*
    distinguishing conservation from, 75–76
    Ed Hillary's ecumenical application of,
        57–71
    as guardianship, 171–72
    Ian Murray on value-laden meaning of, 29
    increasing national focus on, 18–19
    John Panoho's tips on understanding, 23–24
    Kaikoura community's commitment to, 82
    OE (Overseas Experience) prompting
        return to, 142–43, 144, 153
    pay-it-forward sensibility of, ix, 13
    preservation of customs and culture
        elements of, 74
    as social construct, 103
    sustainability element of, 44, 168
    Wanaka Homestead built in keeping with,
        43–44
Kaituna River, 8*p*–11
Kaiwhatawhara Stream, 150
Kapiti Island
    birdlife found on, 156–61
    kiwi population found on, 164
    photograph of, 159*p*
Karakia (Māori prayer), 10
Karori Wildlife Sanctuary, 136
Karu Tahi (water monster), 195
Kauri tree forests, 213–16
Kawa Kawa (New Zealand pepper tree), 84
Kawarau River trip, 17–19
Kayak/kayaking, 144–45
Kaye, Michael, 53
Keenan, Sarah, vi
Kendall, Thomas, 210–11
Kennett, Jonathan, 151
King, Stephen, vi, 212–16
Kipling, Rudyard, 48
Kitamura, Hijiri, v
Kitchingham, Lynda, 105, 108

Kiwi bird population, 163–65*p*
Kiwi expedition (Colorado River), 14–15
Klassovity, Paul, 196, 198
Kleel, Dick, 106–07
Kleinman, David, vii
Knowles, Chris, 133
Knowles, Julia, 133
Koopu, Haromi, 187–88
Koru (newborn fern), 175*p*
koruru mask, 150*p*
Krakauer, Jon, 178
Kramer, John, vi, 15
Kupe (great Polynesian explorer), 218

Lafferty, Steve, vi
Lahood, Bruce, v
Lake Ohakuri, 188
Lake Rotomahana, 185
Lake Taupo, 180–81
Landcare Research–Manaaki Whenua, 201
Laugesen, Karen, vi
LeBon, Nadia, vii
Le Maire, Jacob, 51
Levin, Debbie, ix
Lighthouse (Cape Te Reinga), 228*p*
Logan Brown (restaurant), 141–44
Lord of the Rings (film), 131
Luke, Andrew B., v, 138

McQueen, Maureen, 150–51
Main, Annette, v, 170, 171
Mana (power, spiritual strength), 74,
    186–87
Manawatu, Heather, vi
Manawatu, Maurice, vi, 82, 83–91, 103
Māori carvings
    paua (abalone) shells used in, 147*p*
    traditional *koruru* mask, 150*p*
Māori culture. *See also* Kaitiakitanga

belief in all things as part of, 227

contacting John Panoho to examine the, 21–23

contemporary tourism as dumbing down the, 22

on kaitiaki (human agent), 77

kaitiakitanga on preservation of, 74

lack of environmentalism of early, 14, 33

limited and judicious use concept of, 105

on *mana* (spiritual strength), 186–87

meaning of community in, 40

OE (Overseas Experience) prompting return to, 142–43, 144, 153

storytelling used to preserve, 161–62

taonga (treasure) of, 36, 37

weapons of, 76*p*

whakapapa (oral genealogy) of, 83–84

whales honored by, 100

on when to share sacred knowledge, 123

worldview of, 35–38

Māori myths
    on birds as spirits, 167, 226
    creation story, 34
    Hinenuitepo (goddess of night and death), 88–89
    on Karu Tahi (water monster), 195
    on kauri tree and sperm whale, 214
    Kylie's stories on, 34–38
    Maui-tikitiki-a-Taranga (or Manui), 27–28, 87, 88–89
    Maurice's tales of, 87–91
    on Mount Aspiring, 37*p*
    on origins of Wairakei Terraces, 183–84
    on Paikea ("The Whale Rider"), 82–83, 98
    on pounamu (greenstone), 74, 81–82
    Tāne (a god), 89
    Tangoroa (lord of the sea), 98
    on Warrior Mountains, 174

Māori people

Boyd massacre (1809) by, 190–92

disease scourges affecting the early, 210

early Christian missionary efforts among, 210–11

early Western explorers on the, 127–28, 189–92

growing political influence of the, 139

historic decline and population of, 154

lack of environmentalism among early, 14, 33, 213, 216

loss of traditions among, 161–62

"Pōkarekare Ana" (love song), 146

Te Reo Māori language of, 162

traditional food and hospitality of the, 145–46

Treaty of Waitangi (1840) impact on, 153–54

Māori song (sung by Kylie), 38

Māori Tours Kaikorua, 83

Marine Mammals Protection Act (1978), 93

Maritz, Paul, v, 1

Marlborough Sounds
    early history of, 125
    exploring beauty of, 125–33
    New Zealand wines produced in, 123, 128, 132

Marlborough Sounds Adventure Company, 125

Marsden, Samuel, 180, 189–90

Maui-tikitiki-a-Taranga (or Manui) [demigod], 27–28, 87, 88–89

Meridian Energy, 139

Merkle, Molly, vii

Methane emissions, 180

Millburg, Steve, vii

Miller, Richard, vi, 209–10

Moa (flightless bird), 33

Moffat, Steve, vi

Mohi, Hinewehi, 162

Motuara Island (wildlife sanctuary), 127*p*

Mountain Travel Sobek, 261

Mount Aspiring, 34*p*, 37*p*

Mount Aspiring National Park, 25, 28, 42*p*

Mount Cook (Aorangi), 58*p*–71*p*

Mount Everest, 63

Mount Tarawera eruption (1886), 184–85

"The Mouth of War," 209

Mugabe, Robert, 2

Mulgrew, Peter, 197

Murdoch, Shaun, vi

Murray, Ian, 25–26, 28–29, 135, 222, 225

Mussel Boys Restaurant, 132

Mutu, Vanessa, vi, 21

MV *Te Aihe* (catamaran), 160*p*

Myer, Martyn, 31

National parks
    Mount Aspiring National Park, 25, 28,
        34*p*, 42*p*
    Tongariro National Park, 177

NETCOR (New Zealand Education and
        Tourism Corporation), 187

*New Zealand: Being a Narrative of Travels
    and Adventures during a Residence in
    That Country between the Years 1831
    and 1837* (Polack), 167

New Zealand. *See also* Aotearoa (land of the
        long white cloud)
    conservation policies of
        development of modern, 76
        DOC official approach to, 105, 107, 138
        managing paua (abalone), 141–42
        Marine Mammals Protection Act (1978)
            on, 93
        protecting dolphins, whales, and fish
            resources, 102–07
        sustainability goals of, 203–07
    demographics of, 11*p*

Department of Conservation (DOC), 105,
        107, 138

Department of Tourist and Health Resorts,
        186
    history of
        early Western exploration of, 48–50, 125,
            127–28, 189
        geological, 26
        Māori oral tradition, 83–84, 161–62
        whaling industry, 93, 219*p*
    kauri tree symbol of, 213–16
    Māori myths on birth of, 27
    OE (Overseas Experience) of residents,
        142–43, 144, 153

New Zealand nikau, 133*p*

New Zealand wines, 123, 128, 132

Ngapora, Kauahi, vi

North Island
    early European settlers of, 222
    early whaling around, 218, 219
    Hokianga Harbor, 218–23
    kauri trees left on the, 213–16

North, Roger, vi, 40–44

"Number eight fencing wire" mentality, 222

Ocean of Kiwa, 226

OE (Overseas Experience), 142–43, 144, 153

Okarito Lagoon, 73

Oral tradition
    to preserve Māori culture, 161–62
    whakapapa (oral genealogy) of, 83–84

Otari-Wilton's Bush, 149–52

Paikea ("The Whale Rider"), 82–83, 98

Panoho, John, vii, 21–24, 40, 142, 162, 167–68

Papatuanuku (mother earth), 34

Paraparaumu beach, 156

Parker, Dorothy, 123, 128

Parks, Tricia, vii

Paua (abalone), 141–42
Paua shell art, 147*p*
Peirce, Everett, v, 5
Peirce, Tom, 1, 4*p*–5, 167, 194, 223, 225
Peterson, Carey, vi
Pharazyn, Linda, vi, 120–22
Pharazyn, Simon, vi, 120–22
Pincott, Ricky, vi, 135
Pōhutukawa tree (Cape Te Reinga spirit tree), 226
"Pōkarekare Ana" (love song), 146
Polack, J. S., 167
Poroporo (nightshade plant), 84–85
Potts, Thomas, 81
Pounamu (greenstone), 74, 78, 81–82
Poutini (giant water being), 74
Powell, John Wesley, 17
Propellerless river craft, 47*p*
Puckey, William, 225

Queen Charlotte Sound, 126
Queen Charlotte Track, 129, 131–32
Queenstown, 25*p*–26

rāhui (Māori management technique), 105
Ramakrishnan, Shantini, vii
Ranginui (the sky), 34
RENAMO genocide (Mozambique), 2
Ridgeway, Rick, 223
Ris, David, vii
Rollinson, Dan, v, 149, 152
Royal Forest and Bird Protection Society, 105
Ruwhiu-Karawana, Kylie, vi, 33*p*, 34–38, 167

Schulte, Dick, vii
Seymour-Smith, Justin, 2
Sheep industry, 180, 201
Sims, Ed, v, 199, 201
Single-gable marae, 154*p*

Slow Food movement, 145
Smith, George, 129
Smith, Lisa, 129
Smith, Thomas Brent, 102–03
Sobek, 4
Solomon, Darcia, 106
Sophia, 185, 186
Southern Alps (South Island), 65*p*
South Island
    early British exploration of, 50
    exploring beauty of, 14–17
    Kaikoura of, 93, 99–100, 110–13, 116–18, 120–22
    Kawarau River trip, 17–19
    Mount Cook (Aorangi) of, 58*p*–71*p*
Southern Alps, 65*p*
South Island saddleback, 125
Species extinction, 33
Stokes, J. L., 61
Sulfur-crusted pits, 185*p*
Sustainability
    kaitiakitanga as, 44, 168
    New Zealand's goals regarding, 203–07

Tama ki te Rangi (Māori chief), 81–82
Tāne (a god), 89
Tāne Mahuta ("Lord of the Forest"), 211*p*, 214–15
Tangaroa, Niko, vi, 172–76
Tangoroa (lord of the sea), 98
Tan, Raewyn, vi
Taonga (Māori treasure), 36, 37
Tasman, Abel Janszoon, 48–50
Te Papa Tongarewa (Our Repository of Treasures), 152, 154*p*
Te Rākau, Hāmi, vi, 74–78
Te Rākau, Pauline, vi, 74
Te Rauparaha (Māori chief), 161, 163
Te Reo Māori language, 162

Terraces, Wairakei, vii
Te Taniwha, Horeta, 189
Tieke Kāinga, 175
Tobias, Chris, v
Tolkein, J. R. R., 131
Tompkins, Kelly, vii
Tongariro National Park, 177
Tongariro Power Scheme, 172
Tourism
    Department of Tourist and Health Resorts
        New Zealand, 186
    Edenic myth as part of contemporary, 44
    factors driving, 206
    haka (Māori war dance) adapted for, 161–62
    helicopter tours, 31–32
    Māori culture dumbed down by, 22
    whale watching, 93–100, 112
Treaty of Waitangi (1840), 153–54
Trees for Travellers, 116–18

Waipoua Forest ("The Dinosaur Forest"), 212*p*
Waipoua Forest Trust, 212
Wairakei Geothermal Power Development,
    186
Wairakei Terraces, 181*p*, 183–85
Waka Tours, 173
Walking with Dinosaurs (TV series), 188

Wall, Stevie, VI, 10, 11
Wanaka Homestead, 40–44
Wanganui, 170
Warrior Mountains, 174
Watson, David, 125
Wellington
    energy resources used in, 135–39
    Otari-Wilton's Bush, 149–52
    Te Papa Tongarewa (Our Repository of
        Treasures) New Zealand. *S*in, 152, 154*p*
Wellington Harbour, 135, 139*p*
whakapapa (oral genealogy), 83–84
The Whale Rider (film), 98
Whale Watch fleet, 97*p*, 99, 100
Whale watching, 93–100, 112
Whaling industry, 93, 219*p*
Whanganui River, 173
Whare Kea Chalet, 23*p*, 29, 32*p*
Wills, Gavin, v, 15*p*
Wills, Lucy, 16
Wilton, John, 149
Wood, Anne, vii
World Wildlife Fund for Nature, 104–05
Wright, Chapin Jonathan, 223

ZORG (Zero Organic Waste), 112

RICHARD BANGS HAS OFTEN BEEN CALLED the father of modern adventure travel. He has spent 30 years as an explorer and communicator, and along the way he has led first descents of thirty-five rivers around the globe, including the Yangtze in China and the Zambezi in southern Africa.

Bangs has published more than one thousand magazine articles, sixteen books, and a score of documentaries. He also founded Sobek Expeditions, which in the early 1990s merged with Mountain Travel to become Mountain Travel Sobek. His recent book *The Lost River: A Memoir of Life, Death and the Transformation of Wild Water,* won the National Outdoor Book Award in the literature category. He is currently producing and hosting the PBS series *Richard Bangs' Adventures with Purpose,* with companion books from Menasha Ridge Press.

For more information, visit **www.richardbangs.com**.

Future New Zealand explorer Jasper Bangs